MW01166164

# Polish Greats

# Polish Greats

**Arnold Madison**

J
920
Md

David McKay Company, Inc.
New York

**Library of Congress Cataloging in Publication Data**
Madison, Arnold.
  Polish greats.

  Includes index.
  CONTENTS: Jadwiga. —Nicholaus Copernicus. —Tadeusz
Koscinszko. [etc.]
  1. Poland—Biography—Juvenile literature.
[1. Poland—Biography]  I. Title
CT1230.M28      920'.0438 [B] [920]      79-3462
ISBN 0-679-20876-3

1 2 3 4 5 6 7 8 9 10
Manufactured in the United States of America

For David Lee Drotar, who traveled with this book from the beginning to the end.

# Contents

# 1

# Jadwiga

One person who holds a special place in the hearts of all the Polish people is a queen who ruled for only fifteen years and died before she was thirty. In a way, she is often viewed as the "Polish Joan of Arc," for she was dedicated solely to one great cause. She was also deeply religious and, like her French counterpart, was proposed for sainthood.

Jadwiga was born in 1370 to Louis the Great and the queen mother, Elizabeth of Bosnia. The king had already made plans for the young girl and her two sisters, Maria and Catherine. Jadwiga would marry William of Hapsburg, son of Leopold III of Austria. The eldest daughter, Catherine, would inherit Poland upon the king's death. Unfortunately, Catherine died before Louis, so he decided Poland would go to his second oldest child, Maria. Again, Louis was wrong. Immediately after his death, Maria through marriage, was raised to the throne of Hungary. Therefore, the queen mother proposed that Jadwiga become the new ruler.

A majority of the Polish nobility were in agreement with this proposition. But, even before the eleven-year-old Jadwiga was enthroned in 1834, her life was being determined by the powerful nobles in Poland. They certainly did not want their country connected with the German states, so William of Hapsburg was totally unacceptable as a husband for the new ruler. But they did have a candidate: Jagiello, Grand Duke of Lithuania. Secret negotiations were immediately begun.

The political maneuverings came to a head in August, 1385, transforming Cracow into a city of intrigue. Because William had learned of the nobles' plan to have Jadwiga marry Jagiello, he rushed to Cracow to save his love from the "barbarian."

The Polish lords prevented him from even seeing the girl, knowing that Jadwiga preferred her Hapsburg prince as a husband. While some representatives met with envoys from Jagiello, others discussed the plan with Jadwiga. If she would agree, they urged, the treaty signed with Jagiello would be the most important one in Poland's history.

Slowly, the enormity of the projected goal was grasped by the young girl. Truly, the future of her country depended upon her. Nothing must come before Poland.

The agreement — formally approved in Krewo, Lithuania, in 1385 — was a major step forward for Poland. Jagiello guaranteed to unite Lithuania and his Ruthenian lands to the crown of Poland forever. Ruthenia occupied territory then held by Hungary and Russia. The union provided both nations with a common access to two seas: the Baltic and the Black Sea. The ports and the combined strength of two nations would enable Poland to resist domination from the Russians in the east and from the Germans in the west. There was another article in the treaty that made an even stronger impression upon the religious Jadwiga. Jagiello promised to convert his dynasty and nation, the last pagan country in Europe, to Catholicism.

In February, 1386, Jagiello arrived in Poland for his baptism and marriage. During the former ceremony, he received the name Ladislaus. On February 18, 1386, twelve-year-old Jadwiga married the Lithuanian Grand Duke. Two weeks later, his coronation was celebrated.

Jadwiga had been crowned "king" in 1384, but now she became a coruler. And she was a coruler in the fullest sense of the word, for Jagiello wisely sought her guidance, having recognized her character, intelligence, and cultural background. Jadwiga supplied a true desire for peace and a spirit of moderation in state decisions. For example, when relations with the Teutonic Order of German Knights were tense, Jadwiga entered the discussions as a mediator, bringing about peaceful resolution.

True to his word, Jagiello, who seemed to have undergone a moral uplifting through his baptism and association with Jadwiga, introduced Catholicism to Lithuania in 1387. Throughout her short reign, Jadwiga believed the Polish-Lithuanian union should not be one of mere treaties and agreements but a joining based on true spiritual fellowship. To build this goal into reality, she undertook the renovation and the reorganization of the University of Cracow.

The university, founded in 1364 by Jadwiga's uncle, Casimir the Great, had physically fallen into decay and financially into debt. The money problems could be easily resolved. Without the slightest hesitation, Jadwiga donated her jewels to the university. But creating a center of study was more difficult because she wanted the university to be the greatest one ever devoted to religious instruction. The model would be the brilliant theological department of Sorbonne College, at the University of Paris. Plans were examined, modified, and approved in order to make a world of Catholicism available to the students of Lithuania and Poland.

Tragically, Jadwiga would not live to see the tribute to her faith. During 1399, she became pregnant. Hope ran high through the united countries for a son. Casimir the Great, although he had married three times, had produced no male heirs, and neither had Louis the Great.

Jadwiga's child was a boy, but the happiness was short lived. The baby died shortly after birth.

Weak from the pregnancy, as well as saddened by her son's death, Queen Jadwiga never regained her strength. She died in 1399 at the age of twenty-six, one year before the doors of the new University of Cracow were opened.

Truly deserving of sainthood, Jadwiga had shown the Polish people, through her own deeds, the need for equitable compromise and a devotion to faith.

# 2

## Nicholas Copernicus

One particular person was to benefit from Jadwiga's dream of a new University of Cracow and to bring unexpected glory to the institution. This man would originate a revolutionary theory in astronomy and would become an outstanding mathematician, linguist, and Greek scholar.

On February 19, 1473, a son was born to Mikolaj Kopernik and his wife, Barbara. The father was a merchant and a magistrate in Torun, a town in eastern Poland, and he bestowed his own first name on the youngster.

During his early years, young Kopernik did not seem especially destined for greatness. He enjoyed playing along the banks of the Vistula River, and he did fairly well at school. Upon the death of his father, ten-year-old Kopernik was adopted by his maternal uncle, Lucas Watzelrode, a priest, who decided that his nephew would enter the church, too. Appropriately, after completing his schooling in Torun, Kopernik enrolled in the University of Cracow for his theological studies. During these years, he also adopted the Latinized form of his name: Copernicus.

At the famous institution, he listened as the older generation protested against the growing belief that the earth was a sphere. If that was so, they claimed, the rivers on the underside would fall from their beds and every stone would drop into space. But, while at Cracow, Copernicus also heard the stunning news that Columbus had returned from his voyage. The ships had not sailed off the world's edge, nor had the great serpent, supposedly inhabiting the ocean, swallowed the vessels.

Copernicus had already begun to devote thought to another classic problem—that of tracing mathematical order in the movements of the heavenly bodies. The generally accepted explanation of his day was one that dated back to Ptolemy of Alexandria in the second century A.D. Ptolemy maintained that the earth was the center of the universe, with the sun, planets, and stars revolving around the earth.

In 1496, Copernicus traveled to Italy, where he studied canon law at the universities of Bologna and Padua, and received his doctorate at Ferrara. While there, he was exposed to the early Greek theories of Aristarchus, who lived in the third century B.C. Aristarchus suggested placing the sun at the center of the universe. Along with his religious and mathematical instruction, Copernicus received medical training at Padua. He then spent another year in Rome pursuing those studies.

In 1506, Copernicus returned from Italy and went to Heilsberg as a physician to his uncle, who was now the Bishop of the Prussian diocese of Ermeland. His uncle helped his nephew obtain an appointment as a canon in the diocesan cathedral of Frauenburg. Upon his uncle's death in 1512, the thirty-nine-year-old Copernicus assumed his duties in the city on the Baltic Sea. In his new position, he demonstrated that he knew more than canon law, medicine, and mathematics. Copernicus proved to be the stuff of which heroes are made.

From 1519 to 1522, hostilities flared between Poland and the Teutonic Knights. Frauenburg fell to the knights, and the canons fled to Danzig. Copernicus was appointed the commandant of the Allenstein fortress. The fortified retreat became a refuge for all those fleeing the knights.

Using the cathedral's money, Copernicus bought cannons to defend his outpost. The action resulted in a sharp reprimand from his superiors. Ironically, those same people came to Copernicus when the enemy lay siege to Allenstein, begging him to hold that last bulwark for at least three weeks. Under the command of Copernicus, the fortress survived until peace was achieved.

Copernicus continued to exercise his power as a statesman even after the conflict ended. He drafted a plan to prevent inflation. The proposals for remedying the postwar debasement of money were presented before government officials. Unfortunately, his idea of establishing a standard value for money was too bold for the ordinary mind, and the theory was never put into practice. He prayed that he would fare better with his astronomical theories.

While living in Frauenburg, Copernicus studied the night sky from the wall surrounding the cathedral. His instruments were handmade, according to Ptolemy's directions. He recorded his calculations and theories, planning to publish them in a book titled *De Revolutionibus Orbium Coelestium*. In the text, he wrote: "The theory of the Earth's motion is admittedly difficult to comprehend, for it runs counter to appearances and all of tradition. But if God wills, I shall in this book make it clearer than the Sun, at least for mathematicians."

Unfortunately, God did not so will. *De Revolutionibus* was divided into six books. The theory that the earth revolves on its own axis as well as around the sun, like the other planets, was amazingly accurate. But Copernicus had failed in his figures detailing the planetary orbits, and he was especially inaccurate about Mars. Today, the reason is known for his failure. The planets' orbits are not circles, as Copernicus thought, but ellipses. And the path Mars travels is the ellipse that deviates the most from a circle. But Copernicus could not believe that God would create anything except the most perfect form for a planet's route: the circle.

Although only a portion of his work was incorrect, Copernicus was discouraged and shelved the book. Word of his theories spread, however, and both praise and ridicule were heaped upon him.

Being a Catholic, Copernicus knew the Pope's opinion would be vital in making a decision to release a published record of his observations. The Pope listened to a lecture on the Copernican system, and a cardinal sent a secretary to obtain copies of Copernicus' records. The cardinal wrote an accompanying letter with his request to see the charts and figures. "If you fulfill this wish of mine, you will learn how deeply concerned I am for your fame and how I endeavor to win recognition of your deeds."

Although the letter encouraged Copernicus to work on the final chapters, the cardinal's death prompted him to return the book to the desk drawer. The aging Copernicus decided he would take the book to his grave.

But fate had other intentions. Two events happened almost simultaneously when Copernicus was in his late sixties. First, a bishop in a neighboring diocese urged Copernicus to publish his great work. As if awaiting his cue, a disciple of the Copernican system, who taught astronomy in Wittenberg, arrived at the home of Copernicus. Georg Joachim von Lauchen had at first ridiculed the deductions, but then he became tremendously interested in their importance.

Studying the pages, von Lauchen was most excited about the scientific information, and even wrote a summary of the first chapters. This was released in 1540. He begged Copernicus to allow the book to be printed, because the observations must not be lost to the world. Basking in the enthusiasm of the young mathematician and perhaps wanting some tangible evidence of his studies to be left behind, Copernicus surrendered the manuscript to the man. Von Lauchen then sent it to a Nuremberg printer.

While the book was on the presses, Copernicus became ill. A printed volume was sent to its creator while he lay on his deathbed. In his final hours, Copernicus was able to hold in his hands the ideas that would one day lead to men walking on the moon.

Nicholas Copernicus died on May 24, 1543, at the age of seventy. Not only did the Copernicus theory live on, his life gives inspiration to others who seek to bring about change. The ignorant usually ridicule concepts that are in opposition to current thinking, but those who rebelled against Copernicus were the educated—the most difficult enemy to overcome. Copernicus demonstrated that one individual with faith in a dream can change the world.

# 3
## Tadeusz Kosciuszko

Oddly enough, one person who would help the common people on two continents in their struggles for freedom was born into the nobility on February 14, 1746. Tadeusz Kosciuszko was the son of a small landowner. Even though his parents were not wealthy, their small claim to noble blood would enable their son to climb up through the military ranks.

Kosciuszko first attended the Piarist college in Lubieszow, then the military academy in Warsaw. While training with the cadet corps, his leadership ability and intelligence attracted the attention of King Stanislaus II, who decided to develop Kosciuszko's talents with state-funded training.

In 1769, he was sent to Paris, where he studied the art of fortification as well as painting. Although the two fields seem disparate, there was a definite connection, because an architect of military defenses must be able to reproduce those concepts on paper.

Returning to Poland in 1774, Kosciuszko was hired by a Cossack leader, Jozef Sosnoski, to teach drawing and mathematics to his daughters. Unwisely, Kosciuszko made the mistake of falling in love with the youngest girl, Ludwika. The couple's plans to elope were discovered by the girl's father, and Kosciuszko managed to escape with only a minor gunshot wound. He had to flee not only Poland, but Europe, to be safe from the enraged father.

In the summer of 1776, Kosciuszko volunteered his services to the American Continental army, which badly needed someone with the training that Kosciuszko had received. For developing the means of defending Philadelphia, he was elevated to the rank of colonel of engineers. His assistance at Fort Ticonderoga, in what is now upper New York State, contributed directly to the defeat of General John Burgoyne in the Battle of Saratoga. This setback was a crucial one for the British, and it prevented them from capturing the strategic colony of New York. During 1778 and 1779, Kosciuszko designed and built the fortress of West Point, which stands today as the West Point Military Academy.

Still his skills continued to aid the struggling colonists. In 1780, Kosciuszko became the chief engineer of the Southern forces, and he took part in the sieges of Ninety-Six and of Charleston. In appreciation for his tremendous assistance, Kosciuszko was granted United States citizenship, a large annual pension, land, and the rank of brigadier general.

For many men, this might signal a time to retire to a leisurely life, but not for the thirty-eight-year-old Kosciuszko. He returned to his native Poland in 1784, and lived in the country, but his rural existence ended five years later. In 1789, when the Polish army was being rebuilt, Kosciuszko was commissioned as a major general. On May 3, 1791, the constitution was proclaimed, and the man was back in battle — again fighting for freedom. But the tide of battle went poorly, and King Stanislaus surrendered to the pro-Russian confederation. Kosciuszko, along with other officers, resigned his commission and retired to Leipzig.

But the desire to free Poland was not finished. Kosciuszko traveled to Paris in an effort to enlist French aid for a Polish army that might reclaim their land. Although he had many changing reforms to present to the French, they did not wish to finance a revolution. By the time he returned to Leipzig, he learned that a rebellion had already begun, and that Russian forces were sweeping in to smash the insurrection. Accepting an offer to head the Polish army with dictatorial powers, Kosciuszko hurried to Cracow.

On March 24, 1794, his guns and ammunition were consecrated, according to a church tradition. This gave the insurrection religious sanction. The number of rifles was low, however, and the commander recruited peasants, armed with scythes and pikes. Kosciuszko hoped that their burning passion for freedom would compensate for their lack of arms.

On April 4, 1794, Kosciuszko scored a stunning victory over the Russian forces at Raclawice, and hopes soared about the revolutionists' ultimate success. But the auspicious beginning failed to deliver its promise. On June 8, a Polish division was defeated at Chelm. By the middle of the month, the enemy occupied Cracow, and Kosciuszko was forced to retreat toward Warsaw.

The Russian and Prussian armies united, aiming a thrust for Warsaw. Their force of 40,000 well-trained and heavily armed men would be met by Kosciuszko's 20,000 soldiers and 18,000 armed civilians. Perhaps the general's belief that the desire for freedom can defeat greater odds was true, because his men held off the enemy until the besiegers withdrew on September 6. Elsewhere, however, his generals were being defeated, one by one. On October 10, Kosciuszko attacked the Russians at Maciejowice, but his army of 7,000 was almost decimated by 14,000 enemy soldiers. Seriously wounded and unconscious, Kosciuszko was taken prisoner on the battlefield.

Transported to St. Petersburg, he was imprisoned in the Peter and Paul Fortress. Released on November 24, 1796, Kosciuszko traveled through Finland and Sweden, arriving in London on May 30, 1797. The people there gathered to honor the brave man who had done so much for liberty, even though some of those efforts were against British forces during the American revolution.

Pleased with his reception, he realized he had to sail on to America to claim his pension, which had been accumulating during his absence. Not only did he need money, his dream of a free Poland needed backing. His funds had been building up in the United States to the amount of $18,940. Kosciuszko, the true believer in liberty, had Thomas Jefferson sell the lands given to him in gratitude. With the money from the sale, Kosciuszko bought blacks—but not for slaves. As soon as he had purchased the enslaved people, he set them free.

Although Kosciuszko did not realize the fact, his

fighting days had ended on the bloody battleground in Poland. He moved to France, where he repeatedly tried to enlist aid for another Polish rebellion. Throughout Europe, people turned away from his requests, and Kosciuszko retired to Solothrurn, Switzerland. There, on October 15, 1817, the gallant fighter died. His body was returned to the land he loved and had struggled so valiantly to free. With due honor and praise, Kosciuszko was placed in the Cracow cathedral, where his tomb remains to this day.

# 4
## Count Casimir Pulaski

Another Polish general, who believed firmly in freedom and whose path crossed that of Kosciuszko, was Count Casimir Pulaski. In many ways, their lives were similar.

Casimir Pulaski was born on March 4, 1748, two years after Tadeusz Kosciuszko. Like Kosciuszko, Pulaski was a child of wealthy landowners. The family estate was set like a jewel in the rolling hills southwest of Warsaw. "Winiary," as the property was called, had a huge white house, with thick, decorative columns. There the boyhood years of Pulaski were spent in relaxed, carefree play. But swirling around him was a steady stream of talk about Poland's freedom. Casimir absorbed his father's intense national feelings, sensing a thrill of pride when a parade passed with a Polish banner flying.

At first, he was taught by a governess and a tutor, but when he was six years old, Pulaski attended the local parochial school, where he was an average student. In 1759, Casimir moved on to the school of the Teatyni Fathers—an institution that was not noted for its high scholastic achievements or for strict discipline. Pulaski enjoyed the next four years, and had become an adept dancer and a cultured gentleman by the time he graduated at the age of fifteen. His father was more interested in developing Pulaski's devotion for Poland than building his mind, so he next sent his son to the palace of Prince Karl of Courland.

Although Pulaski had received no military training, he engaged in a minor skirmish with the Russians during his stay at Courland. The battle whetted his appetite for a military career and taught him much about the Russian people and their tactics. He now began reading and studying any material he could find about arms, military training, and battle strategy. Although he did not see any means of putting those into action, he was certain that one day he would join the fight for Poland's freedom.

The moment came sooner than he expected, and from a place he had not anticipated. When he was nineteen, his father and brothers decided to organize a rebel army, and Casimir was to be the person to train them. The troops were called the Knights of the Holy Cross. Slowly, during 1767 and into early 1768, bands of men by the fifties and hundreds arrived at "Winiary" to be molded into an efficient force.

During the year, Pulaski became an itinerant general. To train all the Knights in one location would attract the unwanted attention of the Russians, so the family used the many farms owned by Pulaski's father. Groups of would-be fighters gathered and awaited Casimir's arrival. Once

Pulaski had taught the soldiers the basics, he left them under the charge of experienced officers and moved on to the next farm.

Late in February, 1768, the decision was made to bring the entire army together in the ruins of an old fort. The site was deep in Poland, in the small town of Bar. Slowly, the Knights arrived, until nearly six thousand men had assembled.

During the next few months, Pulaski led his forces on guerrilla attacks and in small battles with the Russians. In June, however, Casimir and his men were trapped in a monastery near Berdyczow. Surrendering against the insurmountable odds, Pulaski was taken prisoner. But the Russians did not want to execute him as a traitor because he had become such a folk hero to the people; a massive revolt might occur if Pulaski were sentenced to death. He was exiled to Turkey but continued making attacks into Poland. However, a final defeat wiped out his forces, and he had to flee to France.

In 1777, he volunteered his services to Benjamin Franklin in Paris. When his offer to fight in the Continental army was accepted, Pulaski sailed to America. There, on September 11, 1777, he distinguished himself during the Battle of Brandywine. His reward was a commission as a brigadier general. The man now had the rather strange title of Brigadier General Count Pulaski.

Early in 1778, Congress approved his plan to raise an independent cavalry army. Pulaski certainly had knowledge along those lines. Drawing on his experience with the Knights in Poland, he gained the support of the common people, who wished to aid the struggle for freedom. Although his officers were mainly French, German, and

Polish—a fact that distressed many colonists—the enlisted men were German farmers from Pennsylvania.

During the same year, Pulaski's legion engaged in minor battles in New Jersey. While Pulaski was encamped at Trenton, he had a surprise visitor—another Pole. Kosciuszko joined his fellow countryman for a few days. Neither man knew they would never meet again.

The Continental Congress ordered Pulaski and his men to Charleston in May, 1779. Their arrival was most opportune because they strengthened the sagging American forces defending the city against a British attack. The residents had been urging the American forces to surrender, but Pulaski's men spurred their morale, and British General Alexander Prevost's army was repulsed.

The Polish Brigadier General and the British General encountered each other again the following October, when Prevost's army was firmly entrenched in Savannah. The plan was for the French fleet to move into the harbor and form a blockade, while Pulaski attacked and surrounded Savannah from the land. Although the plans contained solid military strategy, the British had been alerted to the method of attack.

The battle was fought bravely, but briefly. Many Americans were wounded or killed, including Pulaski. He received a serious wound in the left groin, which knocked him from his horse. As a gesture of respect to Pulaski's courage, General Prevost ordered a cease fire until the Americans could carry their wounded leader off the field. Pulaski was first taken to a temporary shelter and then brought aboard the *Wasp*, an American warship.

Although American doctors and the best doctors from the French fleet tried to help Pulaski, he weakened steadily and slipped into a coma. The *Wasp* was docked in Charleston harbor as people waited, fearful that death would be the final outcome. Brigadier General Count Casimir Pulaski died on October 9, 1779. The weather had turned unseasonably hot, and gangrene had spread throughout his body, so the thirty-one-year-old leader was buried at sea.

Casimir Pulaski, although he had lived a short life, left many memories behind: not only his military actions on behalf of his own people, as well as of the American colonists, but also his generous contributions of money to the colonists and his awakening American generals to the need for a better cavalry.

Like his fellow-countryman, Kosciuszko, Pulaski hated tyranny. His real enemy was not Russia or England, but those men who sought to keep others enslaved. And for Pulaski's efforts to spread freedom, both Americans and the Polish people revere his memory.

# 5
# Adam Mickiewicz

While others were demonstrating that the drive for freedom was an integral part of the Polish people, it remained for Adam Mickiewicz to express those dreams in poetical form. Even today, he is considered Poland's greatest poet.

Mickiewicz was born on Christmas Eve, 1798, in Azosie. From 1815 to 1819, he studied at the University of Vilna, accepting a teaching position at the *Gymnasium* in Kaunas upon graduation. Even after he began work as an instructor, he returned frequently to Vilna, for those university years had been formative ones for the poet. Not only had he perfected his writing craft, he had developed a political consciousness. In 1817 he had joined a secret student organization and now wished to keep those contacts. The work for a free Poland had to go on.

In 1822, Mickiewicz's first book of poems, *Poezye, I*, was published, followed the next year by *Poezye, II*. Unfortunately, Mickiewicz's deep feelings about Poland were too evident in his poetry. Later in 1823, he and other members of the secret group were arrested by the Russians. At their trial, Adam Mickiewicz was accused of "spreading wrong-headed Polish nationalism," and he was exiled to Russia.

Provided with a nominal government job as a means of support, Mickiewicz went to St. Petersburg in October, 1824. He then was moved to Odessa. Although he was in foreign, if not enemy, land, Adam Mickiewicz continued his writing and often met with other poets and writers in St. Petersburg. A leading Russian poet, Aleksandr Pushkin, befriended him.

While living in Russia, Mickiewicz created an epic poem, *Konrad Wallenrod*. The work supposedly portrayed the wars between Lithuania and the Teutonic Order, but in actuality it represented the feud between Poland and Russia. The poem was published in 1828, and the Polish people understood its meaning immediately.

Due to ill health, the poet requested a passport to leave Russia. After traveling through Germany and Switzerland, Adam reached Rome in November, 1829. There he lived for a year, basking in the mild climate and working on various compositions. A year later, the news of the Polish insurrection of November, 1830, reached him. But, for some unknown reason, he did not embark for Poland until the following April. (Possibly he did not want to risk his health in the fierce Polish winter.) At any rate, he did not reach the region of Poznan until mid-August 1831 — too late to engage in the fighting because, within a few weeks, the Russians were to seize Warsaw. Remaining in the country only a few months, he moved on to Dresden with other Polish emigrés. Although their mood was depressed, grieving for their fallen comrades and crushed dream, Mickiewicz continued work on the third part of a poem that had appeared in his second collection: *Dziady III (Forefathers' Eve)*.

Although not evident in that poem, subtle changes were taking place within the poet. Religion, previously important, was becoming a dominant factor in his life. In August, 1832, he settled in Paris and began writing in biblical prose. From 1832 to 1834, he wrote his great epic poem, *Pan Tadeusz*, which has religious overtones. The poem does contain humor, but it is a most serious composition. It portrays the effect the Napoleonic myth had on honest and simple people, who saw the emperor as an instrument of God. A line states the people's feelings: "God is with Napoleon —Napoleon with us."

During this same period, Mickiewicz met Celina Szymanowska. She was truly a soul mate, possessing the same sincere religious feelings as he.

In July, 1834, Adam and Celina were married, and together they formed a lay religious society for prayer and meditation. But this spiritual feeling within him would change in the next few years.

In 1839, he was appointed a professor of Latin Literature at the University of Lausanne, but resigned that position in 1840 to accept the chair of Slavonic literatures at the College de France.

A climactic meeting occurred in July, 1841. Mickiewicz was introduced to Andrzej Towianski, a mysticist. The man was enormously persuasive, and soon had the Polish poet completely imbued with his beliefs. These philosophies began creeping more and more into Adam's teach-

ing. The university first warned him not to teach those
doctrines, then finally suspended Mickiewicz in May,
1844. However, he continued to be under the sway of Towianski until 1848, when he wrenched himself free. In
making the break, however, Adam was temporarily
without a goal. His early years had been filled with the
dream of Polish freedom, then religion, and, finally, mysti-
cism. Now where?

Mickiewicz returned to his earliest goal: a free Poland.
In January, 1848, he headed for Rome, hoping to persuade
the Pope to support his aim of national liberty. While in
Italy, Adam saw the outbreak of the Italian revolution as a
stepping stone for his plan. He organized a small military
unit to fight alongside the Italians against the Austrians.

Secretly, he viewed this small force as the nucleus of the
army he would employ to free Poland. But his scheme
failed, because when he returned to Paris to enlist the aid
and funds of other Polish nationalists, the fighting force
disintegrated. Another hope was dashed. Even worse was
the fact that Mickiewicz had written little poetry since
1837. He tried slipping back into literature by editing a
radical newspaper, *La Tribune des peuples.* This only
alienated Napoleon III, who now fired him completely
from the College de France. Poland's greatest poet then
became a librarian.

The Polish people, however, seemed to need his guidance once again. In September, 1855, Prince Adam Czar-
toryski sought Adam's services as a mediator. Would Mickiewicz go to Turkey and work out an agreement between
the factions of Poles preparing to side with the allies in the
Crimean War? Eager to be of service to his people, the
fifty-seven-year-old Mickiewicz and his wife departed for

Constantinople. Unfortunately, before he was able to complete this latest attempt to assist the Polish people, fate blocked his plans.

Adam Mickiewicz died in Constantinople on November 26, 1855. His body was returned to France and buried in the Polish cemetery in Montmorency, near Paris. Thirty-five years later, his remains would be brought to the country he had loved all his life and be placed in a vault in the Cracow cathedral.

Although his life appears to be a pattern of unfulfilled goals, and paths that led only to dead ends, Adam Mickiewicz earned the love of his people, not only for his dream of a free Poland but for his poetry and writing, which was filled with romanticism and strong emotion. While the subjects and forms of his poetry were often new, the meaning was always clear. This small but powerfully written legacy of literature is a fitting tribute to a man of many dreams.

# 6

# Frederic Chopin

On February 11, 1810, with all due pomp and circum-
stance, Napoleon I married Marie Louise of Austria, thus
further cementing the growing French empire. Meanwhile, in a small village about eighteen miles west of
Warsaw, another Frenchman, Nicholas Chopin, and his
Polish wife awaited the birth of their second child. Ironically, the couple's first child bore the name of Napoleon's
bride, Louise, and Nicholas may have noted that fact when
he heard the news from his native country.

Born and raised in the French grape-producing province
of Lorraine, Nicholas left France when he was sixteen
years old. He was accepted as a steward to a Polish count
and fought in the Polish National Guard against the Russians in 1794. Nicholas eagerly adopted his new land and,
in 1806, married Justyna, a farm girl. The husband and
wife moved into a cottage on the Skarbek estate, owned by

Justyna's distant but wealthy relatives, who hired
Nicholas as a tutor. Each day, Nicholas taught the Skarbek children, while Justyna marketed and kept their cottage tidy and neat. The rooms had raftered ceilings, the
beams decorated with garlands of painted flowers. Outside, real blossoms grew in the colorful garden, bounded
by a rippling stream. Numerous trees relieved the
monotony of the flat, dark plains that stretched to the
horizon.

In this pastoral setting, Frederic Chopin arrived on
March 1, 1810. Prophetically, the boy was born to simple
parents on the estate of an aristocratic family. His greatest
musical achievements were to be based on the peasants'
mazurkas and the polonaises played at the majestic
dances of rich people.

Frederic's father had already realized the need for a
larger income before his son's birth. When the boy was
only eight months old, the family moved to Warsaw, where
Nicholas taught French at the Lyceum and, later, at the
School of Artillery and Military Engineering.

Isabella and Emilia, Frederic's younger sisters, arrived
in 1811 and 1812 respectively. For nightly amusement,
everyone gathered around the piano while Justyna played
the mazurkas she had known from childhood. At an early
age, Frederic revealed a talent for mimicry, being able to
imitate practically any person, and his family performed
small skits and plays for their own entertainment. During
these early years, familial warmth and common interests
were bonding Frederic and his sisters with deep emotional
feelings.

In addition to his acting ability, Frederic displayed a
remarkable sensitivity to music. Merely listening to a

haunting melody played by his mother would bring tears to his eyes. No one actually suspected, yet this was the first indication of a brilliant talent that would make one word—Chopin—synonymous with great music.

First came mere tinkering with the piano keys. Then, before he was six years old, Chopin began to pick out simple melodies and compose music. Piano playing became such an integral part of his life that, at the age of seven, Chopin was allowed to begin formal lessons.

Zywny, his instructor, was actually a violinist, but he was a well-rounded musician who appreciated traditional music by Mozart and Beethoven as well as the more modern compositions of Hummel. The natural arm and wrist flexibility and agile fingers of Zywny's student compensated for the lack of systematic teaching techniques by the instructor. Rather than the usually tedious piano lessons endured by so many youngsters, Chopin's sessions with Zywny were like social get-togethers between two friends—one seven years old, the other sixty-one. Seated side by side, the pair *discovered* music amidst laughter and conversation. Their relationship deepened into a friendship that existed long after the piano lessons ceased.

Already, Chopin's musical talent was beginning to be noticed. His first published composition, a polonaise in G minor, was printed when he was seven. One year later, he was playing at private soirées. In that same year, 1818, an important breakthrough came for the budding pianist when he was invited to perform at a charity concert. Bedecked in a velvet suit with a large lace collar, Chopin seated himself before an audience and played a difficult concerto by Gryowetz. When the fervent applause died down, Chopin was greeted by his mother, who asked him what the audience had liked the best. The eight-year-old boy replied, "My collar, Mama."

The passing years slowly produced other demands, which prevented total absorption with music. Until now, Chopin had been tutored at home by his father. This permitted him to devote a major part of his time to the piano. He was not bereft of friends his own age, however, because several boys from the country lived in the house while school was in session. In 1823, the thirteen-year-old Chopin enrolled in the Lyceum, and academic subjects, such as Latin, received temporary priority; music became secondary. The fun-filled hours with Zywny ended. Chopin did develop a degree of fluency in Latin, but spelling was his downfall then, as it was to be his entire life.

Settled into school life, Chopin now began private lessons with Joseph Elsner, a famous conductor, composer, and teacher. Although study under Elsner was not as informal as that with Zywny, the training was undoubtedly more beneficial. Elsner quickly detected the streak of romance that characterized Chopin's compositions. He was wise enough not to discourage this trait. In fact, he labelled it genius at one point. But he was strict about the boy's learning harmony and counterpoint. Under Elsner's guidance, the smoldering talent flared into a brilliant flame.

The days now included the Lyceum classes, study with Elsner, and a burgeoning social life. Chopin was invited often to receptions and balls in Warsaw, where he was also requested to perform. The music played at these occasions was the polonaise, the age-old stately dance of the aristocracy. Chopin absorbed the strains and made them part of him. However, the busy hours of each day were affecting his health. He had always been frail, but the strain of study and social events weakened him further.

Each summer, and during school holidays, Chopin vacationed on country estates of friends. There, while enjoying the nourishing benefits of fresh air and activities such as horseback riding, Chopin came to know Polish folk music. He was intrigued by the strange melodies of the mazurkas, dating from a time before European scales and chords had reached that section of the continent. These, too, became part of his repertoire, along with the polonaise.

Although many musicians were composing polonaises and mazurkas as dance music, even while in his teens Chopin's poetic compositions were much too personal to be used in a ballroom or at a rural festival. Perhaps unconsciously, the young composer was drawing upon the traditional dance forms, instilling them with his empathy for the people's suffering and his hopes that Poland would one day be free.

The year 1825 was to be a milestone for Frederic Chopin. First, Czar Alexander I of Russia arrived in the capital city to officially open the Polish Parliament. In 1814, the Congress of Vienna had transferred the Grand Duchy of Warsaw to Russia. Various festivities and concerts were staged during the state visit. At one, Chopin improvised on a new piano organ — the aeolomelodicon — developed by a local instrument maker. The Czar was so impressed by the fifteen-year-old boy's performance that he presented Chopin with a diamond ring.

During that same year, Chopin was appointed official organist for the Lyceum, a small but encouraging achievement. Far surpassing his being a school's organist —

or even his receiving a diamond ring from a Czar — was the publication in 1823 of Chopin's official Opus 1, a rondo in C minor. Although, until this time, his music had been mostly mazurkas or polonaises, Chopin had found Hummel's composition exciting, and he wished to experiment with a musical form with showy runs and trills.

However, the rugged routine of public performances and intensive study with Elsner, as well as preparation for the final examinations at the Lyceum, was a tremendous drain on sixteen-year-old Chopin's energy. In the summer of 1826, the family rushed Chopin and his sickly youngest sister, Emilia, to a spa in southwestern Poland, hoping that the mineral water, fresh air, and long hours of sleep would benefit both of them. Chopin flourished in the surroundings, but music was such a part of him that he could not refuse to appear at two charity concerts to raise money for orphans.

That autumn, Chopin — revitalized and a graduate from the Lyceum — became what he had always wanted to be: a full-time music student. His tutor, Joseph Elsner, had formed the Warsaw Conservatoire of Music. Having been a good but not outstanding academic scholar, Chopin was now a superb pupil. He acquired musical skills and techniques as quickly as they could be taught. But the pride of doing well in a field he loved was diminished by the sad death of his sister Emilia in the spring of 1827. The child had steadily weakened, and died from consumption or tuberculosis. The family drew together, finding strength and comfort in each other.

His family was destined to help Chopin achieve the next important step in his career. Although he was receiving excellent instruction from Elsner, as well as acclaim for his performances, Chopin was convinced that he must study in other countries to gain experiences that Warsaw could not offer him. Therefore, in spring, 1829, his father wrote to Minister Grabowski, requesting a government grant to subsidize Chopin's studies. The application was denied. Determined that the nineteen-year-old Chopin would not miss the needed opportunity, the family saved and sacrificed so he could broaden his musical talents.

First, however, there would be a short summer holiday with former school friends. Arriving in Cracow, Chopin met a publisher who wanted to print his music, if Chopin would advertise it by playing the pieces at a public concert. Chopin scored a tremendous success with his wedding song, *Chmiel,* and, at a second concert, with *Krakowiak Rondo.*

The time seemed right to venture forth into the musical capitals of the world. Vienna beckoned, as did Berlin, Paris, and Rome. But for all his conversation and letters to friends, Chopin seemed unable to take the major step. The problem was Constantia Gladkowska. Chopin was in love and could not bear to be away from the girl. As with most elements in his life, his love aided his music. Constantia was studying singing at the Conservatoire, so his relationship with her increased his interest in Italian opera and in the human voice itself. As 1829 became 1830, Chopin lingered in Warsaw, writing his first nocturnes and two piano concertos.

Another hindrance to his departure was his odd feeling that "When I leave it will be to forget home forever; I feel that I'm leaving home only to die." Chopin was not usually given to spells of depression, but possibly the fact that he would be wrenching himself from his closely knit family and the country he loved may have given the move an overly emotional tone. Finally, a friend agreed to travel with him, so plans were made to depart for Vienna. On November 2, 1830, as the coach passed through Zelazowa Wola, Chopin's birthplace, a small choir was assembled by Joseph Elsner to bid Frederic Chopin farewell. As the choral group sang the last line of Elsner's specially written song, "And so, from the bottom of our hearts, we say 'Good luck wherever you go,'" Chopin left the Poland he cherished. Ironically, the presentiment that had delayed the trip for so long was to prove partially true. He would never return to his native land.

His enjoyment of Vienna was cut short by bleak news from Warsaw: on November 29, 1830, the Polish Revolt erupted. Chopin was tormented by images of his young friends being killed and his family suffering deprivation. His fears grew worse when his travel companion returned to Warsaw, leaving Chopin alone to deal with his grief. Nicholas and Justyna wrote, urging Chopin not to return because conditions were so poor, but he could not remain in Vienna where feelings ran high against the Poles.

In July, 1831, he said goodbye to the city that had once seemed magical in all that it had promised. His first stop was Munich, where he gave a successful concert. He then moved on to Stuttgart. There, the news that Warsaw had fallen to the Russians on September 8 caused greater anguish about family, friends, and homeland. Fortunately, he was able to cross into France, the country that would provide a refuge for the remainder of his life.

Paris seemed to be waiting for the young musician. Chopin found an apartment, overlooking the city. The vibrant life of Paris fascinated Chopin, who wrote to friends about the "splendor and filthiness and virtue and vice." An introductory letter from a Viennese friend led Chopin to Paer, the conductor of the Court Theatre. The twenty-one-year-old Frederic was soon immersed in a circle of friends his own age, who one day would also make musical history: Liszt, Berlioz, Mendelssohn, and Schumann. Not only did the German composers extend invitations to visit them in Germany, but the Russian domination of Poland had caused many aristocratic friends to flee that country. They, too, wished Chopin to be their guest. Therefore, the young man was always surrounded by warm, loving people who wished only to be his friends.

As in many artistic careers, Chopin now faced a decision about the wisest route to pursue. He still dreamed of being a piano virtuoso and performing before cheering crowds. Elsner, however, wanted Chopin to write operatic material, drawing on his knowledge of Polish folk music. Therefore, Chopin abandoned his intention to further study the piano — but his dream of being a pianist took longer to die. The criticisms of his performances constantly reflected the fact that Chopin's playing was too fragile and personal to carry through a large performance hall. Over the next few years, Chopin played less in public and more at private parties.

But appearing in salons and drawing rooms did not bring in much money. By sheer accident, a friend invited Chopin to the home of the Rothschilds, one of the richest banking families in Europe, who wished to hire a piano instructor. Their approval signalled the other influential families to seek Chopin's services as a teacher, and he soon became the most sought-after tutor in Paris. He now had

sufficient funds to live well and even to return the money
his family had sacrificed to send him during the hard
years. Other income compensated for the lost dream of
becoming a pianist. Publishers in Germany, England, and
France were interested in Chopin's compositions—not
only in those pieces he had brought from Poland, but in the
new material he was writing as well.

Chopin's old friends, the Wodzinskas, begged him to
visit them in Dresden. To his surprise and delight, Maria
Wodzinska, a youngster when he had last seen her, was
now an attractive girl of sixteen and an accomplished
pianist as well. Maria and Chopin spent much time together that summer. As a farewell present, he gave her a
waltz in A flat, *La Valse de l'Adieu*. Chopin returned to
Paris, but his thoughts remained on Maria. They sum-
mered together in 1836, and on September 9, Frederic
asked the seventeen-year-old girl to marry him. Maria
was delighted to have such a romantic suitor, and Mme.
Wodzinska was equally pleased about her daughter's possible match. Her only concern was that Chopin's ill health
would cause her husband to oppose the marriage. During
the winter of 1836–1837, Chopin suffered another bout of
serious illness, which created considerable concern in the
Wodzinska household. The letters from Mme. Wodzinska
arrived with less frequency and, soon, did not mention
Maria. The following summer, Chopin was not invited to
the Wodzinska home.

But life had already set in motion a relationship that
would far outweigh anything that Chopin had experienced in his twenty-six years.

Near the end of 1836, Liszt invited Chopin to attend a
get-together at the apartment of Countess d'Agoult.

While there, Chopin first met Aurore Dupin, or Mme. Dudevant, perhaps the most notorious person in Paris. She had taken her two children and left her husband in order to live in a city where she could enjoy total freedom in her own lifestyle. Writing novels under the name George Sand, she shocked even sophisticated Paris by wearing men's clothing, smoking cigars, and having numerous love affairs. The first meeting of composer and author was not auspicious. Chopin later wrote his parents that he did not like her face.

But subsequent meetings indicated that not only did George Sand enjoy his company, she wanted to be his lover. At first, the strictly raised Chopin was shocked at the possibility of such a romance. Sand was persuasive, however, and soon convinced Chopin that conventional morality should not keep them apart. Frederic was fearful of displeasing his parents and also dreaded being the topic of Parisian gossip, so they devised a secret plan. In the autumn of 1838, each left the city separately. Chopin brought reams of manuscript paper, and George Sand took her fifteen-year-old son, Maurice, and daughter, Solange. Their destination was the Mediterranean island of Majorca, off the Spanish coast.

For a while, they flourished in the relaxed, mild atmosphere. In fact, Chopin's health was the best he had enjoyed in years. But one day he accompanied Sand and the children along a rough mountain trail and down steep cliffs to the sea. A fierce storm broke while they hiked, and Chopin arrived home exhausted. Heavy rains fell the next few days, and the only heat in the cold, damp house was a charcoal stove. The weakened Chopin was now coughing so badly that doctors were summoned.

Chopin, Sand, and the children moved into an old monastery, which was no longer in use. By adding rugs and cushions, they were able to make the interior a bit more comfortable, but winter seemed an endless wind-and-rainstorm, and food supplies were delayed by washed-out roads. Weakened, Chopin still had to finish the twenty-four preludes that he had sold to a publisher before leaving Paris. In addition to completing the preludes, he composed two other pieces: "The C Minor Polonaise" and "The C Sharp Minor Scherzo."

Although George Sand was writing her new novel, *Spiridion*, her thoughts lingered mainly on Frederic's health. From first awakening until sleep, his body was wracked by steady coughing.

Arrangements were made to sail to Marseilles, but the cart ride down the mountain was so rough that Chopin had a lung hemorrhage. When, at last, they were in Marseilles, Sand and the doctors nursed Chopin back to health. They then traveled to a country house that Sand had inherited from her father. There at Nohant, more healthy in body and mind, Chopin could reflect on those almost-fatal months in Majorca. Drawing on remembered feelings and a new confidence in his ability, he wrote the strongest music he had ever attempted: the B Flat Minor Sonata, often called the Funeral March Sonata.

In fall, 1839, they returned to Paris. Chopin continued to play for private parties and was even invited to perform at the court of Louis Philippe in the Tuileries Palace. For steady income, however, he preferred teaching. The pupils either came to his lodgings or the wealthy families dispatched a carriage, transporting Chopin to and from their homes.

But the seeds of tragedy had already been planted. Only George Sand and a few close friends fully grasped how even a normal working day tired Chopin. Sand appreciated his genius and wanted as much of his time and strength as possible to go into his music. Therefore, she insisted Chopin summer each year with her at Nohant. Here, in the peaceful surroundings, he wrote his greatest music. A more subtle change, however, was taking place because of Sand's concern about his health. Each day she became more of a mother toward Chopin and less a lover.

The change in Sand's role had a detrimental effect on Frederic. He was certain that her motherly attitude indicated that she was in love with another man. This was not true, but there was no convincing Chopin. To make matters even worse, George Sand had written a new novel, *Lucrezia Floriana*. Friends who knew Sand's penchant for basing her stories on real life, shuddered when they read the novel. The main character was Karol, a delicate but extremely handsome young man. His steadily worsening jealousy eventually killed the woman he loved. Sand insisted that the book was not a depiction of Chopin or of their relationship. But the similarities were too striking. Karol was a Polish name, and the hero resembled Frederic both physically and emotionally.

With the tension mounting among all the members of the family, disaster was only a step away. And Sand's daughter Solange, now eighteen and totally self-centered, was to push the situation to the breaking point. Jilting a local aristocrat, she married a penniless, temperamental sculptor named Clesinger. The couple lived at Nohant with Sand. Although Sand was giving them money, Clesinger created such violent scenes that Sand finally

ordered them from the house. In Paris, Chopin was un-
aware of the furious arguments that had prompted Sand's
actions. When Solange requested money from Chopin, he
immediately consented. However, the mother-daughter
estrangement was so severe that Sand interpreted Chopin's kindness as a personal insult. Chopin and Sand did
not write or speak again.

In March, 1848, both were at a Parisian social gathering
and met on a stairway. They paused, gazing at each other,
but the words of apology and comfort that might have
healed the broken love were not spoken. George Sand
turned, continuing up the stairway while Chopin descended. Through their personal letters to outsiders, each
had revealed how much he or she wanted to be reunited,
but an unwillingness to yield had prevented that.

Thus, at the age of thirty-eight years, Chopin was for
the first time in his life totally alone. His aged mother and
two sisters were in Poland, and George Sand had been
sealed off by a wall of suspicion and pride. To complicate
his life even further, Chopin's income was dropping at an
alarming rate. Revolution had broken out in 1848, and the
wealthy families who had once organized the private parties for his performances and paid his handsome teaching
fees were now occupied with survival.

Frederic Chopin literally became a wanderer. He accepted an invitation to travel to Scotland and to stay with
various hosts who were willing to have the poor but famous composer as a guest. However, the weather and the
crudeness of the people he encountered antagonized him,
and he moved from Edinburgh to Glasgow to London. If
personal problems were depressing him, Chopin was even
more frightened because his musical inspiration had de-

serted him. No ideas for new compositions would come.

On November 24, 1848, Chopin returned to his Paris apartment in such poor physical condition that friends immediately called in several doctors. All they could prescribe for him, however, was a good climate, quiet, and rest. During the next few months, Chopin found the strength to teach a few more lessons and compose two minor mazurkas. Friends such as the Rothschilds were secretly helping to pay his expenses.

Although Frederic tried never to reveal his desperate plight to his family in Poland, his mother must have suspected something was wrong because of her son's fervent desire to have Louise visit him. Justyna sent him 2000 francs. When Louise, her husband, and daughter arrived in August, 1849, Chopin was delighted. He had moved into a large, sunny apartment at 12 Place Vendome to be nearer his friends that coming winter. One friend was Solange, who had, in effect, caused the final break between Chopin and her mother, but whom Chopin still loved. During Louise's visit, George Sand made an attempt at reconciliation in a letter to the woman. But Louise ignored the letter and never told Frederic.

Not even the emotional and financial support of family and acquaintances could stem the ravages of tuberculosis. During the night of October 16 and into the early morning hours of October 17, 1849, Chopin hovered on the brink of death. Gaunt, weak, but calm and brave, Chopin received the Holy Sacraments. His final request was that Mozart's *Requiem* be sung during his funeral. Frederic Chopin closed his eyes, and the passionate, short life was over.

A year later, a monument was erected over his grave, in France, a weeping Muse with a broken lyre, designed by Solange's husband, Clesinger. During the dedication ceremony, a small box of dark Polish earth was sprinkled over the site so that Chopin's soul would find eternal rest.

# 7

# Helena Modjeska

Although Helena Modjeska was to reach a height of fame and theatrical success known by few people, the hauntingly beautiful woman would, in the end, be destroyed by a darkness within her and a decision she never made.

A girl was born to Michael and Josephine Opid in Cracow on October 20, 1840. (Later, the records were changed to read 1844, but this may have been an attempt by a beautiful actress to keep her age a secret.)

From her mother, Helena would inherit her physical beauty. Her father died soon after her birth. Her memory of him, written years later, gives a clue to the talents she may have absorbed from the man. She later described him as having "a warm, unsophisticated heart, a most vivid imagination, and a great love of music."

But his early death placed Mme. Opid in financial

45

straits. The woman had ten children to care for: three from her Opid marriage and seven from a previous one. So, one cannot blame the woman when a wealthy older man, Gustav Sinnemayer Modrzejewski, found her daughter Helena most attractive and began providing funds for her care. Although Helena was in love with young Igo Neufeld, she allowed her mother and aunt to convince her to marry Gustav. Also, Igo could do little for the acting career she desired, and Gustav had money and contacts.

Sinnemayer had been her benefactor for years, obtaining singing and dancing lessons for the attractive girl that he loved. Also, although Gustav and Helena both knew that she was pregnant, the family must not realize the child was Igo's and not Gustav's baby. The hasty marriage, with the premature birth of a son, Rudolph, caused gossip throughout Cracow.

Gustav had been seeing to Helena's training for years, and now felt the time was right for others to view her talent. His first thoughts were of Vienna, Berlin, and Paris. But, on the other hand, he did not want to lose his precious Helena. And that might happen if she began performing in large cities and having attractive male admirers. For that reason and also to allow Helena to escape the vicious gossip she met all over Cracow, they decided to leave for Bochnia, where Gustav owned several apartment buildings.

The decision was a wise one, especially for Helena. In Bochnia, they teamed up with Lobojko and formed an acting company. Helena sang and acted her way through the French light opera *The White Camellia* and Victor Hugo's *Marie Tudor,* and other plays as well. The shows toured the neighboring provinces, and with each performance came more praise for the actress.

And with success came greater dreams for Helena, and the certain knowledge that she no longer needed her elderly husband. Helena headed for Cracow — alone. While there, she was united with Igo, her old lover, whom she had never stopped adoring. Within three years, Helena would again become a mother and, again, the daughter would be illegitimate, fathered by Igo. Still, she could not accept his proposals of marriage.

Helena captivated her Cracow audiences, and her fame spread. The theaters of Cracow, Poznan, and Warsaw revolved around her, for she was their star of the highest magnitude.

In the summer of 1866, Helena performed *Macbeth* in Poznan. Crowds had gathered to catch a glimpse of the famous actress, and the German police were out in full force. At the end of the performance, Helena was carried on the shoulders of the Polish youths who surged into the streets, singing patriotic songs. The approximately five thousand people became more militant and soon armed themselves with sticks and shovels. Helena sought refuge in the City Hall when a riot exploded.

Count Bozenta Chlapowki, who had once seen Helena's picture in a newspaper and had fallen in love with her, rushed to the rescue. Once again, Helena had found a wealthy suitor. Bozenta soon became her steady companion and maneuvered an invitation for Helena to appear at the Comedie Française in Paris.

On September 12, 1868, Helena and Count Bozenta Chlapowski were married in Cracow. As the years passed,

Helena was the toast of the Polish theatergoers, but she had a growing restlessness, a feeling that she should leave Poland and, possibly, even Europe. England or even America might offer a beneficial change.

While Helena mulled over these thoughts and battled her boredom, an invitation arrived from an American, offering her an opportunity to tour the United States. Unknown to Bozenta was the fact that Helena had been corresponding with a Polish novelist living near San Francisco. He spoke of the lovely pastoral life that his farm offered. Conflicting thoughts fought in Helena's mind. Should she leave the stage? Would she be content living on a farm? First, she had commitments to fulfill.

On August 13, 1877, Helena Modrzejewska made her first public appearance on an American stage, playing the leading role in *Adrienne Lecouvreur,* and doing the part in English. To help audiences in the United States, who might have problems with her name, she adopted the name Helena Modjeska.

The audience and critics raved about her performance. The unexpected overnight success caused Helena to make the decision she had been unable to reach before. No, she would not spend her life on a farm with some Polish author. She was meant for the stage, and that was where she would always be. Helena did buy a farm near Los Angeles—both for investment purposes and as a sanctuary when life became too frantic—but now she was off to dazzle the United States.

Crisscrossing the country with Edwin Booth as her co-star, Helena played Shakespeare from West Virginia to Iowa. In the fall of 1883, she formed her own company and toured the United States, playing the roles that people loved the most: Beatrice, Ophelia, Juliet.

Helena and Bozenta became American citizens, but Helena never lost her love for her beloved Poland. At times, she donated her time and talent to raising funds for Polish charities. In 1902, she returned for a visit and even made a spectacular appearance at a Cracow theatre. But awaiting the sixty-two-year-old actress was a confrontation with the past.

One night, wishing to relive her happy moments with the man she had never ceased to love, she wandered along the street where Igo once lived. There she found his mother, aged and with failing faculties. The old woman said she would call her son. Helena was amazed. Was Igo there? "Yes," the mother replied, "he is in the Vistula River. But I know the river is good and will release him."

Slowly, the dreadful reality dawned on Helena. Igo Neufeld had committed suicide by drowning himself in the river. Even more disturbing was the fact that he did so when he learned that Helena and the Count were to be married in 1868.

Helena returned to America and continued touring with her theatrical productions. But the sad news had touched her deep inside. Also, her health was failing. Now her shows had to be spaced to give her time to regain her strength. But there was no evidence of this onstage. If anything, she seemed possessed with dynamic emotion. Audiences would wonder if she was giving too much of herself. A manic quality was evident, not detracting from the play but rather breathing fierce, brilliant life into each performance. People sat breathless, listening to the voice with such great range, spellbound by the large, deep eyes.

Then the energy failed. As if she had literally burned the last of the smoldering fire within her, Helena collapsed. She returned to her house in California and became a virtual hermit. Dark memories of her life overwhelmed her. She would confuse time and people, reliving a particular performance or conversing with people who were no longer alive. Outsiders who came to the house on business frequently heard the name Igo, but the word had no significance for them.

The end came on April 8, 1909. The doctor set the cause of death as Bright's Disease, as well as prolonged complications of the heart.(The latter cause could have had several meanings.) Her body was placed in a Los Angeles vault, then transported back to Poland. On July 17, 1909, the Polish woman who had brought audiences to their feet in wild applause was buried in the old Cracow cemetery.

A former dramatic student of Helena's read the funeral oration, which included these lines: "Queen of the dramatic arts, illustrious queen, rest in peace, after your labor, your trials and your triumphs."

# 8

## Joseph Conrad

On December 3, 1857, a son was born to Apollo and Evelina Korzeniowski, who were living near Berdichev, a small town in the Polish Ukraine. The boy, who would one day call himself Joseph Conrad, was given the lengthy name of Jósef Teodor Konrad Walecz Korzeniowski. His parents called him by this third name, Konrad, which was in honor of Konrad Wallenrod, the hero of an epic poem by Poland's national poet, Adam Mickiewicz. Ironically, the boy, given a character's name in literature, one day would himself be a famous author. Other facts in his heritage were also to provide Konrad with future story material.

His family was divided into two groups, not unusual among the country's Russian-dominated patriots. Konrad's father, Apollo, came from a family of headstrong fighters. The fiery Apollo worked with the Polish underground in an effort to liberate Poland. Evelina came from a family that was equally patriotic, but felt the time was not right to throw off Russian oppression. Her people preferred to survive the best they could until such a moment arrived. So from his earliest days, half of Konrad's family dreamed of freedom, while the other half accepted the bleak reality of occupation. This theme, of people torn by ideas and actuality, would be reflected in Joseph Conrad's novels.

In 1861, Apollo Korzeniowski was arrested by the Russian authorities for conspiracy and exiled to the Vologda prison camp in northern Russia. Surprisingly, the law permitted wives and children to accompany the prisoner. Arriving at the camp, the family was assigned numbers. Apollo became number twenty-one, Evelina twenty-two, and Konrad twenty-three. Conditions in the camp were harsh, but Apollo was allowed to continue his work as a translator. There were no youngsters Konrad's age, no games, no schools.

In 1865, when Konrad was seven, his mother died. The boy's only companion was now his father, who would read aloud from French or English literature. Even at this early age, the boy was impressed by Shakespeare. The theme of a play such as *Hamlet*, where a man is forced into actions against his nature, might have reminded Konrad of his father and his homeland.

When Apollo developed tuberculosis in 1868, he was granted the right to return to his native country for the final months of his life. He selected Cracow, which was then located in the sector of Poland controlled by Austria. When the dying man entered the city, the people worshipped him as a great patriot and filled Apollo's last days with many honors. His funeral was a large public event.

Konrad, an orphan at eleven years of age, went to live with his uncle Tadeusz Bobrowski. The man, who was the brother of Konrad's mother, privately felt that Apollo's underground activities had been childish heroics, with no appreciation of reality. Fortunately, he did not shower his nephew with those opinions. However, the early years had left other marks on the boy. Konrad was often moody and withdrawn. Also, he did not display the attitudes that youngsters usually form when maturing. Although he maintained good relations with his family, he felt no deep love, except perhaps for his uncle. He was raised as a Roman Catholic, but would later become a nonbeliever. School, for the most part, bored him, and he considered the instructors to be inept.

The one area that fascinated Konrad was geography — not the school subject, but his personal readings about explorers. His thoughts were gradually dominated by a strange goal, which was especially unusual for a boy living in a landlocked country. He dreamed of becoming a sailor and going to sea. The family struggled to dissuade him, and Konrad reacted with highly emotional scenes. Finally, Uncle Tadeusz agreed to send Konrad to France, a logical choice because all educated Poles spoke French.

On October 26, 1874, only thirty-eight days before his eighteenth birthday, the young man boarded the train bound for France. Marseilles had been carefully chosen because the city was the largest seaport on the Mediterranean. Right from the beginning, Konrad would adapt to two worlds. First, he slipped into the rowdy world of the lowly seaman — the docks, bars, and brothels — mixing easily with men of different nationalities and temperaments. Yet Konrad also moved in the world of the establishment — the fleet owners, traders, and bankers.

He had an introduction letter to the Delestang family, who owned a merchant fleet. And through this contact, Konrad was offered his first job. He signed on as an able-bodied seaman aboard the *Saint-Antoine* and, in 1875 and 1876, made a number of voyages to the Caribbean.

The first mate of the *Saint-Antoine* was a rugged Corsican, Dominic Cervoni, who ruled a tight ship but won the respect of the men aboard his vessel. Cervoni befriended Konrad, and the young Polish apprentice hero-worshipped the self-confident, experienced sailor. Their relationship could be likened to that of teacher and student, or perhaps that which Konrad had lost at the age of eleven: father-son. Not only did Cervoni teach him sailing skills, he also included the eighteen-year-old in his private schemes. In the spring of 1876, while their ship was docked in Haiti, Cervoni and Konrad hired their own vessel and smuggled guns along the Central American coast.

The adventures were a prelude to another illegal arms operation, which the two men engineered upon their return to France. The Delestangs wanted a ship and crew to ferry guns and supplies to a revolutionary army in northern Spain. Konrad and several friends invested all their money in a sailing bark, for which Cervoni would act as skipper. Cesar, Cervoni's nephew, joined the small crew. The outfit conducted several successful runs into enemy waters, but then Cesar sold the route information to the Spanish authorities. A police cutter intercepted the boat, forcing Konrad and the others to abandon ship and escape on land. Although he had survived the near capture, Konrad returned to Marseilles penniless.

At this point, an event occurred which remains cloaked

in mystery. Early in 1878, Uncle Tadeusz received a tele-gram from a friend of Konrad's. The message indicated that Konrad had suffered a gunshot wound and urged the man to send money as well as to come to France himself. Deeply worried that his nephew was dying, Uncle Tadeusz rushed to Marseilles. He found Konrad with a chest wound, but well on the way to recovery. However, the cause of the injury did create new concern. Konrad had attempted suicide. Always high-strung, Konrad had sur-veyed his life and felt his prospects were hopeless. He had no funds, and a love affair with a girl had just been ended. Also, he soon would not be able to obtain work. The French government did not allow foreign men of twenty-one to be employed if they were subject to military service in their own country. In a few months, Konrad would reach that cutoff age.

Years later, Konrad would change this account and even encourage his official biographer, Jean-Aubry, to utilize the revised version. Perhaps the man's talent for fiction was beginning to color the memories of his early life. Konrad maintained that the gunshot wound was not self-inflicted, but received in a duel fought over the love of a beautiful girl. While this argument is more romantic, the probability that he had tried to kill himself is much greater. Suicide is a theme that arises again and again in Joseph Conrad's novels, and was obviously an act about which he had deep feelings. Whatever the cause of the injury, Konrad now had to take stock and figure out his next step. As can happen with certain people who attempt suicide, the aftershock of the act drives away the depres-sion and creates a renewed determination to succeed.

Just as France had been the logical place to begin his sea

career, there was only one sensible answer to where he should continue his work. The other great European sea power was England. At this time Konrad did not speak or read English and literally had heard it spoken only once when a sailor in Marseilles harbor had yelled, "Look out there!" at him. At the time, he didn't understand the words, but would always remember them as the first introduction to his new language.

Signing onto the British freighter *Mavis,* docked at Marseilles, Konrad sailed to Constantinople and then back to England. He stepped onto English soil for the first time on June 18, 1878. His next job was on a schooner connecting the English coastal cities. Then the *Duke of Sutherland* carried him to Australia.

Working as an ordinary seaman was hard. Months often elapsed between jobs, and even when work was available, the pay was poor. Therefore, in the spring of 1880, Konrad studied manuals of seamanship in preparation for a second mate's examination. When he achieved this rating, he accepted employment as the second mate on a leaky old bark headed for Bangkok. Even before the vessel left England, extensive repairs had to be done.

In 1881, the *Palestine* departed, sailing down the African coast and through the Indian Ocean. The ship then turned north, heading for Java. On March 11, 1883, smoke billowed from the hold. Water was pumped in, and a portion of the coal cargo was thrown overboard. A disaster seemed to have been averted until three days later, when an explosion shook the bark and flames quickly spread. The crew abandoned ship, using the three lifeboats. For hours the men rowed and drifted under a blazing sun. Then, in the distance, they could see the cool green mountains of Sumatra jutting above the ocean.

Adventure seemed to follow Konrad as seagulls trail after ships. A year later, he signed on as the second mate of the *Narcissus,* to sail from Bombay to England. During the voyage, a black sailor died, and a ferocious storm struck in the Atlantic. The *Narcissus* limped into port. On December 3, 1884, his twenty-seventh birthday, Konrad passed the test for his first-mate rating. During the examination, the official posed questions about how the applicant would handle hypothetical emergencies at sea, not realizing that Konrad had lived through so many.

The year 1886 was definitely an important one for Korzeniowski. First he became a naturalized British subject; two months later, he passed the test for a master's, or captain's, license. Another event happened that same year but, at the time, it seemed to have no significance. A popular magazine of the day, *Tit-Bits,* announced its annual short story contest. Konrad wrote "The Black Mate" and submitted the tale as his entry. No one is sure why he turned to writing, except that he was exposed to literature when his father was in exile. Also, the sailing life meant much empty time between jobs. Perhaps Konrad only hoped to get some quick money or possibly merely to test his facility in English, a language new to him. In any case, like all great fiction writers, Konrad drew on that which he knew best: the sea and life aboard ships. Unfortunately, "The Black Mate" did not win the prize.

In August, 1887, Konrad accepted the position of second mate on the S.S. *Vidar,* a steamship trading among the islands of the Malay Archipelago. He made six trips on the

*Vidar,* visiting numerous native villages and tiny ports, where he met a wide array of people—both natives and Europeans—who had succumbed to the islands' charms.

His restless nature eventually encouraged him to leave the *Vidar* and accept the captaincy of the bark *Otago.* The ship's captain had died unexpectedly, and a replacement was needed for the voyage from Bangkok to Singapore. If Konrad had sought a position that would test his ability to cope with troubles, he could not have found a better one. First, the ship's papers were in complete disorder. The previous captain had made no entries and was suspected of stealing the profits. During his last days, the poor man had gone completely insane, remaining in his cabin to play his violin nonstop, while the ship drifted aimlessly.

And other problems existed. The first mate hated Konrad because the captaincy had gone to him rather than to the first mate. The second mate was outstandingly stupid, and the entire crew had come down with cholera. Even after Konrad assumed control, matters worsened. The steward died, and his replacement stole Konrad's savings and vanished.

Finally, the *Otago* set sail in February. Mere miles out of Bangkok harbor, the ship was beset by a calm. With his ship immobilized by the weather, Konrad discovered the previous captain had stolen the vessel's quinine and substituted a useless white powder in the bottles.

At last, the needed wind arrived, and the ship sailed the eight hundred miles to Singapore. From there, the *Otago* moved onto Sydney. Each day brought improved conditions and better relationships among the crew and officers. In all, Konrad would command the ship through thousands of miles of ocean. The company owners were tremendously pleased with their capable captain, and Konrad experienced a pride in his abilities. But, once again, he wanted to move on. Also, the letters from Uncle Tadeusz contained requests that Konrad visit him. The man was old, and Konrad knew that too great a delay might mean his uncle could die before he could visit him. In April, 1889, he resigned as captain of the *Otago* and headed for London.

Arriving in June, 1889, Konrad had to wait for the governor of the Polish Ukraine to grant permission for him to enter. So he took a part-time job at a warehouse firm and wondered how he should fill the empty days of waiting for the return trip to Poland.

One autumn morning, for no apparent reason, Konrad began the first page of a novel, *Almayer's Folly.* Even he later admitted that he did not know why he started writing that first chapter. He had no dream of being a writer and had not even made notes about his experiences. Yet he was drawing on those impressions he had received in Malaya aboard the *Vidar.*

During this same period, tremendous interest in Africa had spread throughout England. The fascination seized Konrad, also, and he applied for a position in the Belgian Congo. His two-month visit to Poland drew a flood of friends and relations, who wanted to hear about his exciting life. Then, in 1890, he set sail for Africa. He planned to stay there for three years, but less than twelve months later he was back in London.

For a budding author, the experience was an excellent education. The oppressive heat and primitive living conditions of the Belgian Congo brought out the worst and the best in people. Firsthand, Konrad witnessed people motivated by the darker emotions of avarice, hatred, and lust. He also saw how other individuals found unknown strength and compassion to deal with the less educated, the sick or the injured. Konrad himself almost joined the ranks of the injured. The canoe, bearing him along the Congo River on his journey home, overturned and dumped Konrad and all his belongings into the swirling, muddy waters. He barely saved the first seven chapters of *Almayer's Folly* —as well as his own life.

As valuable as those African months were to the artist, they were physically and emotionally debilitating for the man. In January, 1891, Konrad returned to London, still plagued by the last tinges of malaria. Then he developed gout. His spirits were at their lowest, and his opinion of people had dropped. He felt isolated and disillusioned. Although only thirty-three years old, he believed his life was over. But, rather than resorting to suicide as he had in Marseilles, he realized that *he* had to change the situation. A stay in a Swiss sanatarium restored his health, and more ship assignments brightened his emotional state and financial condition. In his free time, Konrad wrote several more chapters of *Almayer's Folly,* still seeing the novel only as a means of filling idle hours.

In February, 1894, Konrad received a telegram informing him of his uncle's death. The shock depressed him deeply, even though the uncle's will left Konrad a yearly sum of fifteen thousand rubles. This eased his constant concern about money. Still, he wished to return to the sea—but no job openings appeared.

In desperation, he resumed work on his novel, more as a means of taking his mind off his employment problems than of producing a marketable product. As he neared the end of the project, however, his own interest quickened, and he devoted full attention to the story.

On April 24, 1894, he posted a letter to his cousin in Brussels, announcing the completion of the book. But now he had to have the manuscript checked for English errors and then begin the rewrites. The revision was finished in June, and Konrad cast about for a possible publisher. Mr. Fisher Unwin's firm published a special series of books, called the Pseudonym Library. All the books bore a pen name rather than the author's real name. The idea appealed to Konrad, so he settled upon "Kamudi" from the Malayan word *karmondi*, meaning "rudder."

The manuscript was delivered to the publisher, and Konrad passed nervous weeks of awaiting a decision by searching for another ship. But jobs were difficult to obtain. In fact, although Konrad did not realize it, he had sailed on his last ship assignment.

On October 4, 1894, a letter, stating that the novel had been accepted, arrived. Payment was low—twenty pounds—and the author retained only the French translation rights. Yet he was overjoyed, a rare emotion for the usually melancholy man.

A month later, he met with Edward Garnett, who was to be his editor. During the initial conversation, Konrad mentioned that he would probably never write another novel, because he would soon be returning to the sea. Garnett, who was later to discover D. H. Lawrence, argued that Konrad's experiences must not be allowed to fade away to dim memories. Apparently Garnett was persuasive because, before the year ended, Konrad was already working on *An Outcast of the Islands*.

Another important event occurred that same year, and

like so many major steps in Konrad's life, it at first seemed unimportant. One evening, at a friend's house, he met Jessie George. The girl was fifteen years younger than Konrad, but he was impressed with the simple, straightforward manner of down-to-earth Jessie. Perhaps he did not recognize consciously that these same qualities had characterized his mother, Evelina.

For years, Konrad had worked under the name Konrad Korzeniowski. Although *Almayer's Folly* became too long for the Pseudonym Library, both editor and writer saw a need for a more easily remembered author's name. Thus Joseph Conrad was born when the novel was released in April, 1895. The critical reaction was immediate and overwhelming. Newspapers and magazines claimed that Conrad was a new voice in English fiction. The praise was inspiring for Conrad, but the publishers noticed that the public was not buying or reading the book.

For most of 1895, Conrad worked on his second Malayan novel, tried unsuccessfully to resume his sea career, and courted Jessie George. The man must have seemed a most unusual suitor to the girl. Weeks would pass without a word, and then he would appear unexpectedly, only to vanish again. When he was with her, Conrad was the most gloomy of beaus. He talked constantly of a lingering illness and of the fact that he did not expect to live long. One day, they sought refuge from the rain in the National Gallery, where Conrad proposed to her. He added quickly that they had better marry right away because he would soon die. Ending on the dismal note that he did not wish to father any children, he awaited her answer.

Fortunately, Jessie saw through this facade of melancholy, or possibly she realized that life with this man of many moods would never be dull. She accepted immediately. Consent for the marriage was granted by Jessie's mother, and the couple became formally engaged.

With marriage approaching, Joseph Conrad realized he had to make decisions about his life. He could not be a ship's captain *and* an author. But which should he choose? When *An Outcast of the Islands* was published in March, 1896, Conrad made his decision. He would devote his life to writing. The income from the first two books was meager, but he approached his new career with the same determination he had had when boarding the train for Marseilles.

Joseph Conrad and Jessie George were married a few days after the release of the second novel. Although each had a distinct and different personality, the marriage worked well. Jessie assumed a variety of roles—cook, housekeeper, quasi-mother, typist. She respected her husband's talents and did everything possible to eliminate any distractions that would interrupt his writing. When Conrad became depressed and threw manuscripts into the wastebasket, she removed them when he was not looking and stored them in a safe place.

The newlyweds rented a honeymoon cottage on an island in Brittany, France. There, when not exploring the rocky coast with Jessie, Conrad began writing in earnest. He penned three short stories, which sold to magazines. Again he used locales that he knew best: Brittany, Africa, and Malaya. A third Malayan novel was begun, *The Rescue,* but that was shelved when the ideas would not flow. He started *The Sisters,* another novel, and then dropped the idea for good. Prior to their return to England in September, 1896, he wrote the opening chapters of *The Nigger of the "Narcissus."* In this novel, he drew directly on his own experiences aboard the *Narcissus,* using a black sailor as a major character and a ship ravaged by a storm. Conrad finished the novel in January, 1897.

Joseph Conrad was in a rare position. He had a literary reputation, and the critical appreciation of his work grew even more with the publication of the third novel. Other authors, such as Henry James, H. G. Wells, and Stephen Crane, became admirers and close friends. Ford Madox Hueffer, who later changed his name to Ford Madox Ford, was Conrad's coauthor for three novels. All the individuals who recognized quality writing placed Joseph Conrad among the greats. But no one was reading his books. And without a broadly based readership, the writing income was slim. The lack of public response to Conrad's writing seemed to be a chronic condition. More short story collections, and novels such as *Lord Jim, Nostromo,* and *Under Western Eyes,* drew on his memories of Sumatra and gun-smuggling with Dominic Cervoni. Still, the financial rewards were minimal and debts were adding up quickly.

Joseph Conrad's family was growing, too, with the birth of Borys, his first son, and John Alexander, his second. Jessie now had to keep the youngsters away from their father while he worked or when he was in a bad mood. Conrad often joked that both his sons were born on Tuesday—thus wrecking his work week.

And Conrad *was* working. As far back as 1905, he had struggled sporadically with a novel, titled *Chance.* Devoting almost four years to the project, Conrad finished the book. The story ran first as a serial in the New York *Herald* before it was released as a book in 1913. Ironically, the novel is not one of Conrad's better pieces of fiction. The depth and substance evident in some of his earlier creations were lacking. But, for some reason, this book was to be his breakthrough. The serialization in a major newspaper helped boost the sales, and the volume became a best-seller in the United States. And, in England, the book-buying public suddenly discovered Joseph Conrad. Why an audience, which had ignored a writer who was at his peak, bought the books of an author who was in a decline, is an unanswered question.

Through pure coincidence, the next novel was called *Victory*. The sales of this new novel were even greater than those of the previous book. Using his new income, Conrad brought his family to Poland for a tour of Cracow.

While Conrad relived old memories, Russian troops and those of the Austro-Hungarian Empire began mobilizing. On August 1, 1914, World War I burst like an exploding shell. With the advent of war, postal service with England was severed, and Conrad was unable to receive any money. Nor did there seem to be any way out of Poland. On October 7, the family finally managed to board a train for Cracow, where they transferred to one bound for Vienna. The American ambassador helped the Conrads get a pass through Austrian territory. They crossed into the safety of Italy and were on a Dutch ship bound for England when the Austrian government rescinded the pass. But the action came too late. The famous author and his family had escaped.

The war taxed Conrad emotionally and physically. His son, Borys, was of military age and served on the front. The fear that the young man would be killed preyed on Conrad's thoughts. During these troubled years, he wrote some short stories and a novel, *The Arrow of Gold*. But his gout had worsened so much that his fingers and hands had stiffened, and the book had to be dictated to a secretary. The book sold rapidly and hit the best-seller list.

When World War I ended, Joseph Conrad had much to be thankful for. First, his son came home alive. But, also, his native country was free. Pleasure, however, could not supply energy to a man who was weakening. His last two novels, *The Rescue* (1920) and *The Rover* (1922), painfully revealed the artist's decline.

On August 2, 1924, sixty-six-year-old Conrad spent all day at his desk. At eight-thirty the next morning he suffered a sudden heart attack and died within minutes. Four days later Conrad was buried. The lines written by Spenser, which Conrad had quoted on the title page of his last published novel, were etched into the tombstone:

> *Sleep after toyle, port after stormie seas,*
> *Ease after warre, death after life, does*
> *greatly please.*

# 9

# Ignace Jan Paderewski

Ignace Paderewski achieved a degree of success that few people ever attain in their lives. Not only was he a famous pianist, he also composed music, and he became a leading Polish statesman in the world. Most individuals would be pleased to gain renown in one field, but Ignace handled all three with skill and courage.

His beginnings were simple, being born on November 18, 1860, near Kurylowka. His father worked for a Polish landowner. Although his parents were not wealthy, they set aside whatever money they could spare for piano lessons when their son displayed an obvious talent. At the age of three, Ignace was already playing the piano; by seven he was composing simple melodies. Plans were made and executed. At twelve years of age, Ignace began studying piano at the Warsaw Conservatory, and within four years, the sixteen-year-old boy was financing his instruction by teaching beginning students at the same school.

Ignace became attracted to Antonina Korsak, who was his pupil. They shared a love of music and a devotion for each other. No couple could surpass the happiness these two people experienced on their wedding day in 1880. However, their life together was brief. Antonina died the following year in childbirth. Her death devastated Paderewski, who now filled his days with teaching or reliving those brief, happy days with Antonina. However, a man with his intelligence and drive does not dwell on the past, but thinks of the future that his lovely Antonina would have wanted for him.

Helena Modjeska, the great Polish actress, heard Paderewski play and encouraged him to obtain even more instruction. He had a career ahead of him, she said, and owed it to his talent to follow that goal. Her words motivated the twenty-four-year-old pianist. Traveling to Vienna, he studied from 1884 to 1887 with Theodor Leschetizky. As in his early days, he supported himself by teaching, but this time his students were at the Strasbourg Conservatory.

Then came Paderewski's first public appearances and the initial wave of interest, which burgeoned whenever he played another performance. Within four years, his emotional playing had been heard by four cities: Vienna, Paris, New York, and London. In the English capital, Paderewski drew high praise from the music critic George Bernard Shaw, who labeled Paderewski the leading pianist of the time, remarkable both for his musical skill and for his mind.

Audiences everywhere experienced a mystical quality

when Paderewski was on the stage. His playing was powerful, although not technically perfect. Notes had a way of being dropped when Paderewski performed a piece, but when he sat at a piano there was a definite presence on the stage. And everyone felt drawn and filled with feelings às his fingers brought forth Chopin, Bach, and Beethoven from the piano keys.

Success provided funds to buy a home in Switzerland, where Paderewski lived peacefully between concert tours. The house became a true home in 1899, when Paderewski married Helene Gorska. The warmth of the homelife helped his composing, too. In 1901, his opera, *Manru,* dealing with life in the Tatra Mountains, was presented in Dresden. The Symphony in B Minor was performed in Boston eight years later. That year, 1909, was an important one for Paderewski, for he also became the director of the school where he first studied the piano—the Warsaw Conservatory.

Poland was most important to Paderewski, and that fact was reflected in his music, as well as in other generous deeds. On the five hundredth anniversary of the Battle of Grunwald, he presented the city of Cracow with a monument honoring the Polish victory over the Teutonic Order.

When World War I broke out, Paderewski sought to help his beloved Poland by becoming a member of the Polish National Committee, which resembled a government in exile. This group tried to assist people in Poland as much as possible and also attempted to show world leaders the desperate need for a free Poland. Ignace Paderewski was appointed the committee's United States representative, and he was as effective in pressing the Polish cause as he had been in his piano playing. President Woodrow Wilson gave special attention to Paderewski during 1916 and 1917, when the Polish artist urged the President to use his power and influence to see that an independent Poland was organized at the war's conclusion. So fervent were Paderewski's pleas that Wilson included Poland's freedom in his tentative peace message of January 22, 1917, and stated that as the thirteenth of the Fourteen Points designed to insure a lasting peace.

In December, 1918, Poland faced a new problem. There were two governments. The Polish National Committee, which had operated during the war, was viewed by the Allies as representing the Polish people. Meanwhile, in Warsaw, a provisional government had been organized with Józef Pilsudski as the head. Pilsudski asked Paderewski to form a government composed of experts in their respective fields, who also were individuals vitally concerned about Poland's future and not merely about the success of a particular political party.

Paderewski wrestled with the weighty problems, always keeping his country's welfare in mind. When critics complained, he had the answers for them. The new government was created on January 17, 1919. Paderewski appointed Roman Dmowski as the first Polish delegate to the Paris Peace Conference and himself as premier.

As often can happen after a war, people forget the leaders who led them through the bad times. Paderewski's dream of being elected president of the Polish Republic died because no political party supported him. Perhaps anger still lingered in those political offices because Paderewski had overlooked them when forming a nonpartisan government. Discouraged, Ignace Paderewski re-

signed as premier and returned to his home in Switzerland.

In 1921, at the age of sixty-one, he resumed his musical
career, giving concerts in Europe and the United States.
Formerly, he had been the highest-paid pianist in the
world. Now his concerts supported charities that were
helping war victims.

The years passed, and Paderewski reached the status of
a legend. People around the world knew the name and
connected it with the piano, even if they had never heard a
phonograph record of Paderewski playing or attended one
of his concerts. The man might well have retired to his
home in Switzerland, for he was now almost eighty. But
war erupted again, and once more Poland needed him.

In October, 1939, after the Germans overran Poland, a
government in exile was organized in Paris. Paderewski
was offered the chairmanship of the Polish National
Committee. He accepted and headed the government in
exile from 1940 to 1941. He had to flee Paris when the
Germans came, but worked for the Polish cause until he
died in New York City on June 29, 1941.

Paderewski left a legacy of recorded music and his own
compositions, but perhaps the achievement that most
endears him to people all over the world is the way he
struggled to free his native country.

# 10
# Wladyslaw Stanislaw Reymont

Like many creative people, Reymont spent the early portion of his life continually traveling, as if he was trying to escape his roots. At the end, he would receive the acclaim he sought.

On May 6, 1867, the village organist of Kobiele Wielkie, a town near Lodz in central Poland, and his wife had a son born to them. The early years of Wladyslaw Stanislaw Reymont seemed to indicate that the boy would not be successful. When the time came to continue his education beyond the basic village schooling, Reymont failed the tests required to enter the *Gymnasium*. Apparently, intellectual pursuits were not to be his field of accomplishment.

The restless youth drifted from job to job, working at one for a short time, then feeling the need to move on and do something else. He hoped to find that special work that would make him content.

73

The elusive occupation appeared to be nonexistent, however. First, Reymont worked as a tailor. He then decided that the theatre might offer satisfaction, and he signed on as an actor in a traveling theatrical troupe. Although Reymont did not realize the fact at the time, that experience would reap rewards far beyond the bit parts he portrayed on the stage. He became totally dissatisfied with what he felt was the brash and immoral life of the theatre.

Wishing to retreat from the outside world that gave him no pleasure, Reymont became a novice in a monastery. Perhaps, he thought, the sheltered life would permit an outlet for his deep religious feelings and finally bring him contentment as well. But he found the restrictions too confining, and his desperate need to obtain that vague pleasure, called happiness, drove him into the outside world again. But he also needed funds for food and a place of lodging, so he accepted the menial job of railway clerk.

At the age of twenty-five, he decided to try his hand at an endeavor that had appealed to him off and on for the last few years: writing. He penned a few short stories, destroyed them, and wrote a few more. The second batch seemed to have more life and reality because he was drawing on all the people, events, and emotions he had witnessed and experienced during the restless years.

When the stories were published in 1893, he felt encouraged to experiment with other forms of writing. Reymont had taken a pilgrimage to the shrine of the Virgin Mary at the monastery of Jasna Gora. Perhaps he could capture the experience on paper. *Pielgrzymka do Jasnez Gory,* published in 1895, did indeed re-create the popular religious feelings of the time.

The desire to attempt a large literary work had been growing while his shorter pieces of writing were achieving success. He remembered the theatre group with which he had traveled. His co-performers and members of the audience he had met during that time evolved into characters. Reymont had his first novel, *Komedjantka,* or *The Comedienne,* published in 1896.

Other incidents, faces, and environments provided raw material to the author. *Ziemia Obiecana*, or *The Promised Land,* a novel with a sardonic title, was released in 1899. The story deals with life in the industrial city of Lodz and depicts Poles, Germans, and Jews competing ruthlessly for material gain.

But it was to be a small rural town, much like the one he had fled when he was young, that was to bring greatness to the name of Wladyslaw Stanislaw Reymont. He began working feverishly on the longest literary project of his life. Because the town was to be described through the cycle of seasons, the novel was divided into four volumes. These were published between 1902 and 1909. Those simple villagers he had known during his boyhood became the heroes of the lyrical epic, *Chlopi,* or *The Peasants.* The power and quality of the panoramic novel won Reymont the Nobel Prize for literature in 1924.

So, the man whose restless spirit had driven him from a small town had come full circle, finding that elusive satisfaction by writing about his early home. Now he could rest. From that point on, Reymont lived a private life, and little is known about him except what his prolific writings reveal. On December 5, 1926, Wladyslaw Stanislaw Reymont died in Warsaw at the age of fifty-nine.

# 11

# Marie Curie

On December 26, 1923, a huge crowd filled the amphitheater of the Sorbonne in Paris. The occasion was the twenty-fifth anniversary of the discovery of radium. To further honor the occasion, the French government was presenting to Marie Curie—the surviving member of the team that had isolated the radioactive material—an annual pension of forty thousand francs as a "national recompense." This pension would be inherited by the Curies' children upon the mother's death. Most people in the audience knew this reward had been too long in coming.

A small, slight figure walked onto the stage, dressed in her usual plain black frock. As Marie Curie stepped before the large crowd, which included her three sisters, she must have thought back to all the events leading to this moment of glory. Back to Pierre and the hard years, and back to Poland where it all began.

On November 7, 1867, a fourth child, Marja, was born to Professor Vladimir Sklodowska and his wife. The couple, living in Warsaw, already had three girls and one boy. From the beginning, there were clues that this girl might one day do exceptional deeds. Certainly, her childhood environment was beneficial. Her father was an instructor, as well as a gifted scientist. Mme. Sklodowska, her mother, taught in the same school as the professor and was a talented musician.

At four years of age, the high-spirited Marja surprised the family. One day she was sitting with large cardboard letters, supposedly learning the alphabet. Her seven-year-old sister, Bronya, was struggling through a reading lesson. The agony of hearing the girl stumble on the words and sentences became too much. Marja grabbed the book and read the paragraph without a single mistake. Glancing around at the stunned family members, she misinterpreted their silence as approval. She turned the page and flawlessly read the next one. Then she noticed her father's frown and mother's tears and wondered what she had done wrong. Marja did not understand that her parents, being intelligent teachers, believed that very young children should not be forced ahead academically. They wished their youngest daughter to experience the joys of growing up normally and not to become a child prodigy. From that point on, they allowed Marja to read only one hour a day during her lessons.

Wisely, her parents did not curtail Marja's favorite pastime of gazing into a glass cabinet situated in her father's book-filled study. The shelves bore scientific instruments, such as test tubes, scales, and a gold-leaf electroscope. She did not know what the equipment was used for, but found the apparatus so intriguing that she vowed one day to learn. Professor Sklodowska did say something about "physics," so Marja added that word to her list of things to explore. Even the sound of the word—with the repeated s sounds—appealed to her sense of rhythm.

However, when Marja was six years old, her life and that of the entire family underwent drastic changes. At this time, the Polish people were dominated by Russian rulers, who were determined that the Poles would adhere to the Czar's laws. They even forbade anyone to use the Polish language. Professor Sklodowska was continually in trouble with the authorities because he wanted his brighter science students to be able to pursue their talents and receive further training. At last, the Russian government decided to eliminate this annoying thorn in their oppressive sides by sending him to a different school at a lower salary.

The family moved into a cold, depressing flat. More problems arose when Mme. Sklodowska contracted tuberculosis and needed to spend a year in Nice, France. The family income could barely support the necessary treatment. Professor Sklodowska had lost his lifetime savings of 30,000 rubles by investing in a steam mill that had gone bankrupt. Faced with a lower salary and high medical expenses, the family took in boarders in order to pay their bills.

Not only did the tenants bring income to the family, they brought death. Sophie and Bronya, Marja's sisters, caught typhoid fever from a roomer. Tragically, Sophie died a short time after her mother returned from France, still ill.

Then, in 1877, ten-year-old Marja lost her mother. As heavy as the burden was for the girl, Marja had the sensitivity to realize the loss was even greater for her father. Now the man spent his days and nights in loneliness, fighting the ever-constant fear that the Russian authorities would send him to another school and cut his income even more. Marja was determined that one day she would do something to make his life better, happier. Possibly she could find a small cottage for him in the country, where he would sit, smoke his pipe, and read his beloved books.

The professor's library had now become Marja's main interest. With the death of her mother, all limitations on her reading were lifted. Each night, upon finishing her school studies, Marja carried a volume to the dining table and began reading. Her choices varied from Dickens' novels to scientific works she barely understood. The girl displayed remarkable powers of concentration, because while she read, her brother, sisters, and the younger boarders practiced their school lessons by chanting them aloud.

Her school progress reflected this ability to concentrate and to absorb what she read. In fact, when the dreaded Russian Inspector of Schools arrived to check how well the pupils were learning the Russian language and history, the teachers, knowing that Marja was their best example, chose her to answer his questions.

At the age of fourteen, Marja received a scholarship to enter the *Gymnasium,* which offered a diploma upon the completion of her studies. Now her dreams for helping her family grew even greater. She would help Bronya to go to Paris and study medicine. And Hela, her third sister, would need support to become a singer. To facilitate these unselfish dreams, Marja decided she would tutor rich people in Warsaw in French, German, and Russian.

Upon graduation from the *Gymnasium*, Marja was given a year's holiday to visit her relatives. While spending the winter near the Carpathian Mountains, she hiked each day and developed a complete love of nature, which would remain for her entire life. However, her dream of earning money by private tutoring died quickly. She neatly penned cards— "Lessons in arithmetic, geometry, French, by young lady with diploma. Moderate fees" — and sent them off. Little interest was shown, and those students she did have were dullards, whose parents squabbled about money and delayed Marja's pay. Obviously, another source of income had to be found if she was to help her family fulfill their dreams.

In December, 1885, eighteen-year-old Marja became a governess for a wealthy Warsaw family. The situation was so unpleasant that a month later she accepted another job in a distant province. Teaching and caring for the youngsters during the day, Marja studied math and science on her own, scouring about for every text she could find. Her father assisted by mailing her mathematical problems to test her skills. Warm weather brought renewed opportunities to enjoy the outdoors, but only on a limited basis because her responsibilities and self-study consumed many hours each day.

Then Casimir, the eldest son of her employers, returned from Warsaw University. And, with his arrival, love entered Marja's life. The young couple were distraught when his parents would not consent to their marriage. Casimir wanted Marja to run away with him and marry elsewhere, but this was impossible. Marja was sending a monthly allowance to Bronya for her studies in Paris. Also, once again caught up in the magic of science, Marja was thinking far ahead to the day when she could plan for her own life. She envisioned a scientific career and suspected that Casimir would not approve of such work for his wife.

For three years, Marja struggled as a daytime governess and nighttime student, wondering if she would ever be able to study formally that which she loved most. Suddenly light showed where there had been only darkness. Professor Sklodowska retired on a pension and became a well-salaried superintendent of a reform school. He could now afford to pay Bronya's monthly allowance. For once, Marja could divert her savings into her own future. A year later she returned to Warsaw, working for a family there.

Her evenings were spent in a small building with a big name, the Museum of Industry and Agriculture. The exhibits offered nothing to her. But a small, hidden laboratory, kept secret from the Russians, was her nightly destination. There, for the first time, Marja could conduct her experiments and self-study, with actual apparatus rather than merely through the printed page. What a thrill to measure chemicals accurately and have real test tubes.

During the summer of 1891, Casimir reappeared, but when Marja broached the question of her career, he insisted that his wife should remain at home and raise children. With regret, Marja sent him away.

By October, 1891, Marja's dream had come true. She had saved enough for one year in Paris, and Bronya offered to let Marja stay in the apartment that she and her husband rented. So, with a big wooden trunk labeled with the black initials M.S., Marja boarded a train and rode into history.

Upon enrolling at the Sorbonne, the world-renowned university, Marja was handed a registration card. Pausing a moment at the space for her name, she wrote "Marie Sklodowska" and, from that time forward, would only use the French form of her Christian name.

Marie threw herself into her studies, absorbing every word the instructors uttered. After several months of living with Bronya and her husband, however, Marie decided to find her own accommodations. A barren room in the Latin Quarter was found, and Marie moved her few belongings in there.

Her strenuous routine was enough to wreck a healthy person, and for a rather frail, twenty-four-year-old individual, the schedule was tortuous. But Marie was driven by the most demanding taskmaster—a dream. Rising early in the morning, she studied a few hours and then attended classroom lectures. The afternoon hours were spent in the physics laboratory. Upon completing the experiments, Marie headed for the Sainte-Genevieve Library, which helped students by remaining open until ten o'clock at night. Finally, she climbed the stairs to her cold, dim room, wrapped a blanket around herself, and studied until two o'clock in the morning. Only then did she allow herself the rest she needed so badly.

Unfortunately, she neglected to eat well enough to sustain this schedule, often living several days on tea, bread, and butter. At one point, she collapsed from weakness while working in the lab. Bronya and her husband brought her home with them and fed her meat and vegetables. But that was to last only a few days. Then Marie was off to take the master's examination. If her routine had been physically draining, her work methods were rewarding. Marie scored as the top physics student.

Following a brief summer visit to Poland, Marie was back in Paris by October, 1893. She was asked to make a study of the magnetic properties of various steels. The fee was a pittance, but the experience would be excellent for her career. Her instructor, Professor Lippmann, suggested that a workroom might be available in the School of Physics and Chemistry. An eminent scientist friend worked there. Perhaps Marie knew about him. Pierre Curie?

Marie, as well as every other science student, had heard about Curie's work. He had developed the ultrasensitive Curie scale and, through research with magnetism, had formulated "Curie's law." Marie doubted if Pierre Curie would want to be bothered with her simple experiments, but the professor insisted she join him and Pierre for tea. Marie later wrote about that first encounter:

> When I came in, Pierre Curie was standing in the window recess. He seemed very young to me, although he was then aged thirty-five. I was struck by the expression of his clear gaze and by a slight appearance of carelessness in his lofty stature. His rather slow, reflective words, his simplicity, and his smile, at once grave and young, inspired confidence. A conversation began between us and became friendly; its object was some questions of sci-

*ence upon which I was happy to ask his opin-
ion.*

Marie was impressed with Pierre, and he was struck
both by her attractive appearance and by her scientific
acumen. In fact, Pierre was so taken by the Polish girl that
the following summer he asked her to marry him. Marie
refused. Having been hurt by the blighted romance with
Casimir, Marie was determined never to fall in love again
and to dedicate herself only to her work.

For such a determined person, Marie should have detected the same quality in Pierre Curie. She was worried
about her father and decided to return to Poland, possibly
to remain there as a teacher. Pierre emphatically told her
that she must come back to Paris and continue her work.
Marie relented.

While home in Warsaw, she was barraged with letters
from Pierre, and he was there when she stepped off the
train at Paris's Gare du Nord that fall. Pierre did not limit
his campaign only to Marie. He visited Bronya and her
husband, pleading his cause. Marie was invited to meet
his parents. The mother and father were coconspirators,
because they begged her to make Pierre's dreams come
true. Pierre won, but so did Marie when she accepted his
proposal. For now she would have love *and* her career.

The wedding took place on July 26, 1895. Professor
Sklodowska and Hela came from Poland for the joyous
occasion. Honeymooning on bicycles, Pierre and Marie
enjoyed the glorious sunny weather on French roads. They
slept in small inns and discussed nature, science, and their

love in meadows and woods. By August, they arrived at the Chantilly villa that Bronya had rented for the summer. The family group was warm and loving, and Marie's father and sister joined them, along with Pierre's parents and brother, Jacques.

The newlyweds set up housekeeping in a small, three-room flat, which could only be reached by four steep flights of stairs. They each worked during the day, and Marie used nighttime hours for study. A year passed, and their daughter, Irene, was born. But discoveries were being made that were soon to envelop the Curies.

The German physicist Roentgen had discovered X-rays in 1895. Antoine Henri Becquerel, the French scientist, wanted to see whether such rays were given out by fluorescent bodies under the action of light. He experimented with the salts of a rare metal, uranium. To his amazement, he learned that this material emitted rays spontaneously. News of these achievements appeared in scientific journals and papers, intriguing the Curies. Marie especially wished to investigate these fascinating rays.

A ground-floor shed at Pierre's school was made available to Marie. The place was dreadful for scientific work — hot and airless during the summer, cold and windy in the winter. But the adverse conditions meant nothing to Marie. She had a place to work, and work she did. First she determined that, although the rays emanating from uranium were weak, nothing affected them. She wondered if other materials gave off such rays and, testing numerous samples, found that thorium emitted rays. Marie coined the term *radioactivity* as a name for this property. But one point puzzled her. The degree of radioactivity in certain ores was not directly related to the amount of uranium or thorium present. Slowly, an awesome fact dawned. There was a new element contained in those ores, one unknown to science at that time.

Excited, Pierre now joined Marie in her quest. They had discovered that pitchblende ore had four times the radioactivity that pure uranium possessed. But pitchblende had been known for a long time and had been carefully analyzed. If there was another element in that ore, the amount must be minute indeed.

In July, 1898, three years after their marriage, the Curies made another important breakthrough. Not only one new element existed, but two. The characteristics of the first were more easily determined, and Pierre allowed Marie the honor of naming it. She selected *polonium* in honor of her native country. But a new problem had arisen. If they were to isolate two new elements from pitchblende, an enormous amount would be needed. Where would they obtain the money? They were already financing all this work through personal funds.

Marie found the solution. Pitchblende was mined in Bohemia, where uranium salts were extracted to be used in glassmaking. The remaining material was discarded. What if the other two elements were still present in the processed pitchblende? A request was made to the mine operators to sell them pitchblende at a low price. The company directors generously donated a ton of the ore.

New accommodations were needed, and a rickety wooden shed in the same school courtyard was given to the Curies. If the former space was poor, the shack was ridiculous. The one stove gave little heat. During the winter, the man and wife were numb with cold. Because numerous leaks caused rain to drip on the scientists, chalk circles were marked on the tables so that precious instruments would not be placed where rainwater might contaminate them.

The investigation was divided into two parts. Pierre would determine the properties of radium, while Marie would obtain the pure salts of the metal. The woman, with her superhuman capacity for work, did the chores of the team. She shoveled pitchblende from the sacks piled in the courtyard, boiled the material, stirred, poured off excess liquids, and obtained increasingly concentrated solutions. As three or four years passed, Pierre, concerned for Marie's health, often asked her to give up the search. They already had made valuable contributions to science. But no, she was going to succeed even in a primitive shack, where she could not protect her apparatus from heat, cold, or coal dust.

Then, one evening in 1902, when Marie and Pierre were at home, she felt strangely restless. She wanted to return to study the results of her latest efforts to isolate radium. Pierre agreed. As they opened the door to the dark room, Marie saw a bluish glow emanating from a row of test tubes. Her four-year search had ended.

With success came personal problems. One month after the discovery of radium, Marie's father died. She reproached herself for not having visited him again while he was alive. There was no reason for her guilt, because her discovery had given him tremendous pleasure in the last days of his life. Marie, who at a young age wished to make her father happy, had done so in the best possible way.

During this same time, Pierre had health problems,

experiencing pains in both legs so severe that at times he could not sleep all night. The doctors considered the ailment to be rheumatism and prescribed rest. But there was still much to be done. Honors had to be accepted. Marie received her doctorate in physical science from the Sorbonne, and the Royal Society of London presented the Davy Medal to the Curies.

Then came the biggest award, the 1903 Nobel Prize. Becquerel and the Curies shared the Nobel Prize for physics for their discoveries in radioactivity. This brought in 70,000 gold francs, which was soon combined with 25,000 francs for Marie's half of the Osiris Prize.

The amount may have seemed large, but the Curies were not free of financial worries. Numerous debts had to be paid and gifts given to friends and supporters over the hard years. Even though Pierre and Marie faced the prospect of always being in need of money, they refused to patent their process for obtaining radium, believing it was against the principles of science.

The interruptions and distractions in their work were immense. Newspaper reporters, colleagues, and sightseers came knocking on their door. The interest increased in 1904, when Marie gave birth to a second daughter, Ève. In addition, Marie was anxious about Pierre's health. The leg pains had continued, and fears of a malignant illness plagued her. Her own physical stamina seemed weakened. She was nearly forty, but she knew she should still have the energy to do all her work. Then an even greater burden was placed on Marie Curie.

On April 6, 1904, Pierre was wending his way through the rain-soaked streets of Paris. Carrying a large black umbrella, he moved from behind a cab into the path of a heavy wagon drawn by two horses. One animal knocked him into the muddy road, and a wheel of the six-ton wagon crushed Pierre. Death was instantaneous.

Upon receiving the tragic news, Marie was to display an attitude that would characterize her over the following years. Cold, remote, she gave instructions for Pierre's funeral almost mechanically. If her stony exterior gave an appearance of utmost strength, close friends and family members knew the desperation she suffered inwardly. One evening, as she and Bronya gathered to burn the bloody clothing Pierre had worn the day of the accident, Marie confided in her sister: "And now, tell me how I am going to live? I know that I must, but how shall I do it? How *can* I do it?"

Marie did it by throwing herself into work and striving to create the dream that she and Pierre had envisioned. The University of Paris asked that she take her husband's place on the faculty. Marie accepted. This was the first time a woman had ever held the revered post.

Famous people who have experienced personal tragedy have a morbid fascination for some. On the day Marie was to begin her lecture series, the hall was filled with students, newspaper reporters, and even society women. Everyone wanted to see this celebrity. Would she cry? A tradition existed for a new instructor to praise the person who had been his predecessor. How would Marie handle that?

Marie walked onto the platform, bowed, and began. "When one considers the progress that has been made in physics in the past ten years . . ."

The audience stared at the woman who spoke in such an

expressionless voice. There had been no mention of Pierre at all. Again, the familiar words surfaced as the people thought about Marie Curie. "Cold." "Remote."

However, the real Marie Curie was neither cold nor remote. She drove herself relentlessly to bring to fruition the radium laboratory that Pierre had wanted for so many years. She worked late into the night and taught during the day. Often she fainted while in the laboratory or at home. She developed an odd mannerism of rubbing her fingers together as if trying to alleviate the painful burns she continually received from radium. Her happiest moments were those spent with her two daughters and Pierre's father, Dr. Curie. The old gentleman had come to live with them when his wife passed away, and Marie could not bear to have the man stay elsewhere after Pierre was killed. Unfortunately, Dr. Curie developed a severe lung congestion in 1909 and was bedridden for the next year. This added more chores to Marie's day, but she never complained. In February, 1910, Dr. Curie died, and once again Marie experienced grief. Still, outsiders described Marie as "cold, remote, mechanical."

More honors and achievements were earned by her diligence. In 1911, she was awarded the Nobel Prize in chemistry. Three years later, the Sorbonne built the Radium Institute, composed of a laboratory of radioactivity, directed by Marie Curie, and another lab for biological research and Curietherapy, headed by an eminent doctor.

The outbreak of World War I brought the Germans dangerously close to Paris. Marie knew the vials of pure radium in her laboratory must not fall into their hands. She placed each in a protective lead shield and brought them by train to a vault in a Bordeaux bank. During the war, she equipped radiological trucks to X-ray wounded soldiers and was a frequent visitor to hospitals, where she worked with the injured. To provide the X-ray vehicles with a trained staff, she organized and taught a course in radiology.

When the war ended in 1918, Marie Curie was fifty-one years old, but the idea of working less never occurred to her. If anything, she plunged deeper into responsibilities. In 1920, Marie experienced a physical disability. Her eyesight was steadily weakening. She hid the fact from her co-workers by marking her instruments with colored dials and using special lenses. Her daughters attended her at public dinners, deftly helping Marie to find the eating utensils. Even during a successful tour of the United States and a meeting with President Warren Harding, Marie was able to prevent the public from learning about her poor vision. In July, 1923, a cataract operation could no longer be delayed. Although the surgery was followed by severe hemorrhages, Marie insisted upon using her eyes for work as soon as the bandages were removed. Amazingly, after three subsequent operations, Marie regained almost normal sight. She would always wear thick glasses, but was capable of doing the most detailed precision work.

The same year brought the twenty-fifth anniversary of the discovery of radium and a government pension. But Marie still worked on. In 1926, her daughter Irene, who now devoted her life to studying radium, married an outstanding physicist, who joined Marie's laboratory. Everything in Marie Curie's life revolved around the laboratory. Even the eventual cause of her death was to be found there.

Each day Marie handled radium, receiving nasty burns and inhaling its gas. A humming noise had persisted in her ears for some time, but now the volume increased. Her blood pressure declined. In December, 1933, an X-ray showed she had a large stone in her gallbladder. Still more symptoms arose: dizziness, weakness, a constant slight temperature. Marie dismissed them as a touch of the flu, while various doctors diagnosed the illness as bronchitis or possibly tuberculosis. They were wrong.

At the age of sixty-seven, Marie Curie died on July 4, 1934, never knowing that she had pernicious anemia. With all her knowledge, Marie did not realize she was a victim of the miraculous substance she had brought to the world: radium.

# 12

## Artur Rubinstein

Strangely, for a child destined to be a world-famous musician, Artur Rubinstein was born into a family where music was assigned a minor role.

On January 28, 1887, Artur was born to Ignace and Mme. Rubinstein in Lodz, Poland. The town, located southwest of Warsaw, held the textile factory that Artur's father owned. Although the Rubinsteins might occasionally attend the Warsaw Opera House, they did so for social reasons more than an appreciation of music.

Artur's early years were lonely ones because his three brothers and three sisters were much older than he. For amusement, as a toddler, the boy enjoyed listening when his sisters had their piano lessons. When the instructor left, Artur crawled onto the piano bench and played by ear the same melodies through which his sisters had struggled. He even paused at the same places where the girls had hesitated while they had turned a page.

When only four years old, Artur would be asked to play melodies for family gatherings. An uncle thought the boy had unusual talent and wrote to the Hungarian-Jewish violinist Joseph Joachim for advice. Joachim suggested that Artur be exposed to as much good music as possible, but not be forced to take formal lessons. But letting the young child experience the joys of hearing great music was not easy. One night, his mother and father took him to a concert. The blaring trombones frightened Artur, and the parents led the crying child from the theatre.

A family trip to Berlin offered a chance for the boy to meet personally with Joachim. After listening to Artur play several pieces on the piano, Joachim said that when the youngster was older, he must study music in Berlin. Meanwhile, he suggested that Artur should learn the violin. A small violin was purchased, but the squeaky, scratchy sounds irritated Artur. In desperation, he smashed the musical instrument. His father disciplined him, but the incident forever ended the violin lessons.

Musicians who saw Artur perform said the boy was a true prodigy because he could play almost anything by ear and his hands could already span the chords. So, when Artur was five years old, the first of several piano instructors began working with him. The female tutor gave up after a few months because he had learned all she could teach him. The second instructor, who was elderly, fell asleep constantly during the lessons. However, the third teacher was helpful, and worked with Artur for two years.

The instruction came to an end when Artur was seven years old. The family suffered a financial crisis because

Ignace Rubinstein's textile factory was in trouble. The handlooms could not compete against the modern machinery used in other companies.

When her son was ten, Mme. Rubinstein took him to Berlin, where they lived with her sister. Again, Joachim came to the rescue. Not only did he donate money toward Artur's musical training, but he convinced three bankers to provide the needed funding. In addition, he arranged for Artur to study with Karl Heinrich Barth, an outstanding teacher. Mme. Rubinstein returned to Poland, and her young son moved into a Berlin boarding house.

Life was lonely in a foreign city, and Artur could speak only a few words of German. But the days were filled with studies, and he did have the wise guidance of Joachim, who also took him to concerts. As others had suggested, the Polish boy was a prodigy with natural talents. For a child, his hands had a wide stretch. His fourth and fifth fingers were strong, and his thumb bent far below the usual angle.

School vacations were always spent in Poland, for Artur loved the country and his native people. The homecoming, when he was thirteen, was most auspicious because he was to perform with the Warsaw Symphony. The concert was a successful one and gave Artur the patience to continue study with Barth.

In the summer of 1904, Artur had the rewarding experience of being invited to the Swiss home of Ignace Paderewski, through arrangements made by Joachim. The revered pianist and statesman was impressed with the young Rubinstein. Listening to and playing with Paderewski, Artur found the dry, unemotional playing of his teacher, Barth, even more unbearable. Finally, when the instructor dominated his pupil's personal life by telling him what to do in his free time and which friends to associate with, Artur made his decision to leave for Paris. He was almost eighteen, and felt he was ready to enter the world of music.

Paris was decked out in all its greenery when Artur arrived in the spring of 1905. A letter of introduction led to an audition for a concert agent, and Artur was soon performing before Parisian audiences. Unfortunately, even though such people as composer Saint-Saëns felt the young man was most talented, concertgoers remained cool to Artur. But associating with rebel musicians like Maurice Ravel and Claude Debussy was a heady experience and counteracted Artur's apparent lack of success.

When his career seemed unable to get moving, an invitation came from the Knabe Piano Company in the United States for Artur to tour that country. The company would pay his expenses. The offer was a direct result of the wonderful weeks he had spent visiting Paderewski. A guest there had heard him and spoken of his talents when he returned to the United States. Artur enlarged his repertoire, booked passage, and sailed for America.

The tour had its moments of success and failure. From Philadelphia to New York City and Boston, some audiences wildly cheered, while others described his playing as "tedious." Following the Knabe tour, Artur signed a contract with the Shubert Brothers and trekked to Cincinnati, Chicago, and Columbus, eating meals on the run and sleeping on lumpy beds. The box office receipts were often slim, and one critic wrote, "Let the next five years bring him some genuine heartache such as befalls the majority of us . . . and Artur Rubinstein will be the greatest of all pianists."

On the return voyage to Europe, Artur did experience heartache. He had always recognized the fact that he was not technically perfect while performing (even Paderewski left out notes), but he believed he could stir his audiences' emotions. Now the critics complained that he lacked feeling.

Once back in Paris, Artur received concert offers with ever-increasing frequency. For a while these were centered in Paris, but then, as his reputation spread, he appeared in Vienna, St. Petersburg, and London. While Artur was in London in 1914, war erupted in Europe. He offered his services to the Polish Legion in any capacity in which they felt he could be used. Shortly, he was serving as a translator in Allied Headquarters. The work involved translating letters and documents. Some correspondence was written by people who had seen the atrocities German soldiers had committed in Belgium and Poland. Artur vowed never to give another recital in Germany, preferring "to smash his fingers first."

Musical appearances were few during the hard war years, but Artur did have a successful tour of Spain. The Spanish queen, Victoria, even donated her own piano for his appearance in Madrid. Leaving enthusiastic audiences behind in Spain, Artur toured South America, the United States, and Europe. After a 1928 performance with the Warsaw Philharmonic, he met the conductor's daughter, Aniela Mlynarski. Though still a teenager, Aniela was a beautiful blonde girl, who created a strong impression. When Artur left Warsaw, he brought with him the mem-

ory of the fifteen-year-old Aniela. He hesitated to write
her, due to the difference in their ages. Later, he heard that
she had married, and he berated himself for waiting so
long. But the marriage did not last. A mutual friend
confided to Artur that the real reason the marriage had
collapsed was that Aniela loved Rubinstein. Although
Artur could not believe that a girl who had been fascinated
with him after one concert appearance would have such
complete love, he visited Warsaw to speak with her.

In July, 1932, Aniela and Artur were married in London.
Artur, who could create strong emotions in his audiences,
had underestimated the swiftness with which a feeling
can grip a person. Aniela had fallen in love with him one
night, and that devotion never deserted her. Nor did the
discrepancy in their years have an adverse effect on the
girl. Artur would soon discover he had found more than a
loving wife in his Nela. In her he discovered inspiration.
Before that awareness grew, they were off on a South
American tour. While in Buenos Aires a year later, Nela
gave birth to a baby girl named Eva.

Being a husband and a father weighed heavily on Artur's thoughts. The music world was going through a tran-
sition. While audiences still sought emotional performances, they were demanding perfection. Technical accu-
racy had never been Artur's strong point. Now pianists,
who were too old or too set in their ways to acquire the
demanded precision, were dropped by the wayside. Is this
what he wanted for his devoted Nela and lovely daughter?
A second-rate performer for a husband? A has-been for a
father? Artur was in his forties. Did he have the stamina
and determination to make the final climb into greatness?

In the summer of 1934, he and his family rented a small

cottage in Saint-Nicolas-de-Veroce, near the Swiss border.
There, in a windowless garage, with the only upright
piano in the village, Artur worked long hours to achieve
perfection. If his spirits sagged, Nela always encouraged
him. He struggled to be exact in tempo and note-perfect.
At the same time, he did not wish to become mechanical,
so he was cheered when Nela praised the beauty of his
playing. By summer's end, Nela's inspiration and Artur's
discipline had raised his talent and ability to a level never
before evident. If Artur had a sizeable following before,
the name Rubinstein would now be known by millions.

Audiences from Paris to Hong Kong — no matter what
their musical preferences — cheered the new Rubinstein.
The concert tours were unending, and so was Rubinstein's
energy. Between trips he cut phonograph records, often
amazing recording technicians with his ability to
withstand long, tortuous sessions. In 1937, he recorded
fifty-six Chopin mazurkas in one sitting for the His Master's Voice Recording Company. The phonograph records
were to help Rubinstein in another way.

Late in 1937, Sol Hurok, the theatrical impresario, per-
suaded a doubtful Rubinstein to tour the United States.
The American public had not been too responsive in the
past, so Rubinstein was concerned about their receptive-
ness now. The first concert with the New York Philharmonic seemed to prove that Rubinstein was right. The
reviews were appreciative, but hardly cheering. Slowly,
however, attendance at his performances increased, as did
critical enthusiasm. His records had built a previously
unseen audience, which now flocked to hear the pianist.
By January, 1938, Rubinstein was a top name.

The outbreak of World War II forced Artur to leave

France and move to the United States. During the war years, Rubinstein played rigorous tours and aided the Commission for Polish Relief. Although his immediate family was growing, with a son, Paul, the war cut off any news about his family in Poland. When information did arrive, the facts were tragic. Of all the Rubinsteins in Poland, only three distant cousins had survived the German occupation.

The birth of his daughter, Alina, in 1945 and John a year later brought Artur much happiness, but could not relieve the pain deep within the man. Rubinstein had not forsaken his vow made during World War I that he would never perform in Germany. If anything, he was now more determined than ever that it would never happen. Because the war had destroyed so many relatives and friends in Europe and because their two youngest children were citizens of the United States, the Rubinsteins became naturalized citizens of their adopted country in 1946.

The years passed, with Rubinstein reigning at the keyboard. Honors and awards were showered on the gifted musician. An honorary degree from Brown University was followed by another doctorate from Yale in 1962.

In 1973, Rubinstein's autobiography, *My Young Years,* was published, and his son, John, starred nightly in the Broadway musical *Pippin.* Father and son shared musical talent but differed in their tastes, for the *Pippin* score featured contemporary music. Even in 1978, when Rubinstein was ninety-one, his RCA Victor record won an "Emmy" award for outstanding quality.

And of this gift, which has thrilled so many people — from family members, when Artur was four years old, to

the Rubinstein concerts in all the world's capitals — Artur
Rubinstein once said, "I was afflicted with music the day I
was born. It is simply my life, music. I live it, breathe it,
talk with it. It is like an arm, part of me."

# 13

## Pope John Paul II

On the rainy afternoon of October 1, 1979, Pope John Paul II stepped through a plane doorway at Logan Airport, Boston, looking slightly tired. The Pontiff descended the stairway and knelt to kiss the ground. His traditional first act when arriving in a new country, it symbolizes the love that John Paul brought to the people. Greeted by Mrs. Rosalynn Carter, wife of the President, the Pope soon learned that the people of Boston and of the entire United States brought their love to shower upon him. Thus, the second Pope to visit the United States arrived in America.

The man who brings an aura of humility to his position had a humble beginning. And those early years provide the other feeling that he exudes — the moral toughness of a survivor.

Karol Wojtyle was born on May 18, 1920, to working-class parents. His mother was a Lithuanian; his father was a noncommissioned officer in the Polish Army. Family and friends nicknamed the boy "Lolek."

Though early photos show Karol relaxed and confident, tragedy stalked his life. When he was almost nine, his mother died. Yet, in those early years and during his teens, he achieved success at whatever he chose to undertake — whether it was studying Latin and Greek classics, playing goalie for the school soccer team, or performing in theatricals.

Friends who knew him in his young years do not remember him as pious, which might have been expected in a future Pope. Various people described him as ruggedly handsome, athletic, popular with the girls, and prankishly defiant of authority. A rumor exists that he was once in love with a girl who died or was killed by the Germans, but there has been no verification of this. If the relationship did indeed exist, it was before Karol became a priest.

Another friend said about Karol, "He seemed to radiate good cheer and conversation — a bit of gossip, a bit of Homer, a quotation in Latin." But others noted the quiet side — a pensiveness, as if he were contemplating thoughts and philosophies.

When his father died in 1942, Cracow was under Nazi occupation. The twenty-one-year-old Karol worked as a laborer in a stone quarry and then in a chemical factory. He also engaged in amateur theatrical productions in the evening, writing some of the plays himself.

Young Karol had two serious accidents, one of which left a physical mark. He was knocked down by a tram in Cracow and suffered a fractured skull. A few months later, a runaway lorry almost crushed him to death. As a result, his shoulders are slightly stooped.

Remarkably, soon after the accidents, he joined an underground seminary in Cracow. Four years later, in 1946, he was ordained a priest. Next, he received a philosophy degree at Rome's Angelicum, a college run by Dominicans. Coming home, he became a parish priest and taught theology at the Catholic University of Lublin.

In 1958, while relaxing on a canoeing and camping trip, thirty-eight-year-old Karol received the news that he had been appointed auxiliary bishop of Cracow. The choice was a wise one because Karol Wojtyle established an immediate rapport with the student population of that city. Then, in 1964, Bishop Wojtyle became the Archbishop of Cracow, five years later he was a cardinal.

In the same year, 1969, Cardinal Wojtyle made his first trip to the United States. In preparation, he had to learn his sixth language, English. He was already fluent in Polish, Latin, Italian, French, and German.

The cardinal again journeyed to the United States in 1976, visiting sixteen cities in which he spoke and read prepared papers.

Upon returning to Poland, Cardinal Wojtyle still held the people's devotion, even though he angered the political leaders. Using his position as cardinal, he harassed government bureaucrats, who in turn tried to make his life more difficult with small, annoying actions. For example, when he returned from a trip abroad and customs officials confiscated his bags, they returned them weeks later with books missing.

Then came those terrible days in October, 1978. The cardinals were recalled to Rome to elect a new Pope, only weeks after having elected a successor to Pope Paul VI. Death had come swiftly and unexpectedly to the newly elected Pontiff.

Once again the world waited to see the telltale puff of smoke, which indicates that a new Pope has been named. Cardinal Wojtyle was chosen, and elected to call himself Pope John Paul II, taking the name of his predecessor.

The reign of the new Pope has affected Catholics and non-Catholics alike. All the qualities that were evident in him before reaching this high office are still present. His interest in sports continues, even to the point where he rearranged his investiture as Pope so it would not conflict with a soccer match on Italian television. His rapport with young people, so evident in Cracow, was confirmed on his recent trips to Poland, Mexico, and the United States. Sessions for young people only are set aside in any visit to another country.

The sincerity of the man hints of great deeds ahead. People look at Pope John Paul II and see a moral conviction. Others see the man who was so overwhelmed that he wept alongside the death wall of the former Nazi prison camp at Auschwitz, and wonder if his role will be that of peacemaker. If that is to be his role in history, then he will be drawing on the centuries-old dream of the Polish people: freedom and peace.

# Index

# Index